# WYE VALLEY &
# THE FOREST OF DEAN

## WALKS FOR MOTORISTS

Peter A. Price

30 Walks with sketch maps

## COUNTRYSIDE BOOKS
NEWBURY, BERKSHIRE

*Countryside Books' walking guides cover most areas of England
and include the following series:*

*County Rambles
Walks For Motorists
Exploring Long Distance Paths
Literary Walks
Pub Walks*

*A complete list is available from the publisher.*

Originally published
by Frederick Warne Ltd
This edition published 1993
© Peter A. Price 1993

COUNTRYSIDE BOOKS
3 Catherine Road
Newbury, Berkshire

ISBN 1 85306 219 7

Cover photograph of the river Wye from
Symonds Yat Rock taken by Bill Meadows

**Publishers' Note**
At the time of publication all rights of way were shown on the definitive maps
maintained by local councils or were well-established permitted routes, but
it should be borne in mind that diversion orders may be made from time to
time and permissions may be withdrawn.

Produced through MRM Associates Ltd., Reading
Typeset by Paragon Typesetters, Queensferry, Clwyd
Printed in England by J. W. Arrowsmith Ltd., Bristol

# Contents

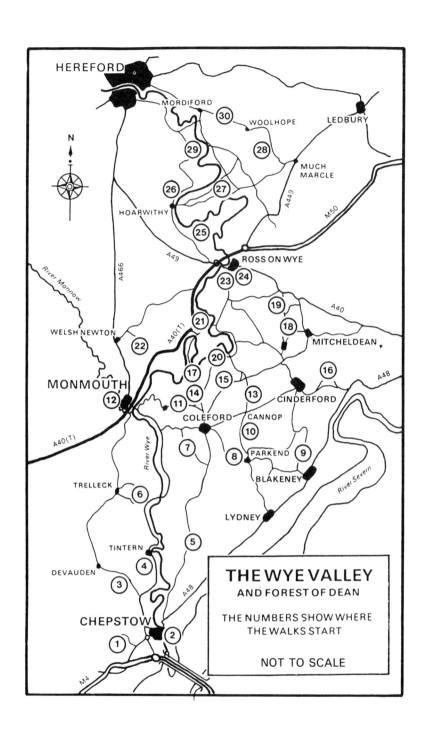

HEREFORD

MORDIFORD

WOOLHOPE

LEDBURY

(30)

(29)

(28)

N

MUCH
MARCLE

(26)    (27)

A449

M50

HOARWITHY

(25)

A49

ROSS ON WYE

River Monnow

A466

(23) (24)

(19)

A40

WELSH NEWTON

A40(T)

(21)

(18)

(22)

MITCHELDEAN

(20)

A48

(17)

(15)

(16)

MONMOUTH

(14)

(13)

CINDERFORD

(12)

(11)

COLEFORD

CANNOP

River Wye

(7)

(10)

TRELLECK

(8)  PARKEND  (9)

(6)

BLAKENEY

River Severn

TINTERN

(5)

LYDNEY

DEVAUDEN

(4)

(3)

A48

CHEPSTOW

**THE WYE VALLEY**
AND FOREST OF DEAN

(1)

(2)

THE NUMBERS SHOW WHERE
THE WALKS START

M4

NOT TO SCALE

# Introduction

The Wye Valley from Chepstow to Hereford is one of the most picturesque regions of Britain. In the southern part the river has cut its way down through 600 ft of rock, so that it now runs in a narrow, tree-covered valley and in the northern part it winds through the lush pastures of south Herefordshire. The whole region has been designated as an Area of Outstanding Natural Beauty.

The lower Wye Valley and the adjoining Forest of Dean are quite unusual and form one of the centres of pilgrimage for geologists from all over Britain. The walks in the northern area described in this book are mainly over Old Red Sandstone. The exception is in the area around Woolhope where the deeper layers of limestone have been pushed up and are exposed.

Until recent years all man's activities have been regulated by his natural environment. The Forest of Dean and the Lower Wye Valley have been the scene of feverish activity for over 2000 years, reaching a peak in the 19th century. Subsequently other regions developed the skills and resources for which 'Dean' had always been famous.

Sitting like a great saucer in a hollow in the old Red Sandstone is a layer of very hard conglomerate rock – nature's concrete. On this is a pile of other saucers – some of hard rock, some of soft, some thick but some very thin. Working up the pile from the conglomerate, the next five are different sorts of limestone. Then there is one of hard sandstone, followed by some 32 made up alternately of soft sandstone and coal. The whole pile has been weathered away so that there is hardly anything left of the top saucers; over millions of years the pile has become irregular and the eastern edges now come up to the surface nearly vertically, whilst the western edges have been pushed down.

When the south of Britain was beginning to warm up at the end of the last Ice Age we know that man was living in a cave on the banks of the Wye near Symonds Yat. That was some 12,000 years ago and man has been in the Wye Valley ever since. Over the years he shaped the countryside to his needs as best he could. Megaliths and mounds, all dating back to the twilight age, are still to be seen, though their purpose is long since forgotten. The presence of eight hilltop earthworks, all within a mile radius just south east of Hereford suggests well established estates. Indeed it is now realised that at the same time that Nebuchadnezzar was king in Babylon there was extensive pastoral settlement on the rich land on the banks of the Wye.

With the Romans came stability and the development of Dean Iron. This was surface mined wherever the ore outcropped in narrow gullies

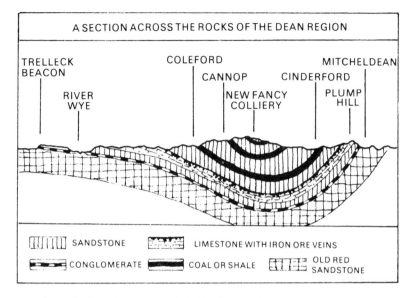

A SECTION ACROSS THE ROCKS OF THE DEAN REGION

TRELLECK BEACON | COLEFORD | MITCHELDEAN
CANNOP | CINDERFORD
RIVER WYE | NEW FANCY COLLIERY | PLUMP HILL

⫿⫿⫿ SANDSTONE     ▦ LIMESTONE WITH IRON ORE VEINS

▬ CONGLOMERATE     ▬ COAL OR SHALE     ▦ OLD RED SANDSTONE

or 'scowles' as they are called. In the north of the area there was a slow but constant change, the result of new farming methods. In the south there was an ever-increasing demand for iron and timber and later coal. The intricate pattern of tramways and railways bears testimony to the energy of the iron and coal industries at the height of their prosperity. Today the north continues its gradual change, with machines replacing human labour, but in the south almost all industry has ended and is being replaced by farming – the farming of trees.

To get the most out of these walks – or any walk – it is necessary to put more in than just walking-power. It is hoped that the observations made along the way will help to make the walks more interesting. Much more could be mentioned, but space will not allow.

All walks in this book are circular. They start and finish at the same place. The routes described are on public rights of way as shown on the Definitive Map or the County Road Record or they are on the Forestry Commission land to which the public have access. 'Members of the Public are permitted to enter Forestry Commission land entirely at their own risk on condition that they will have no claim whatsoever against the Forestry Commission for any loss, damage or injury howsoever suffered or caused.' Some of the walks go through farmland or private woodland that is the source of income to the farmer. Damage to fences, walls or gates – apart from the expense involved in repairs – may cause suffering to animals who could get out and eat the wrong food or be injured by a car.

If you see a fire in the forest put it out if you can – if not, telephone the fire brigade (999).

Make sure you observe the Country code:

Enjoy the countryside and respect its life and work
Guard against all risk of fire
Fasten all gates
Keep your dogs under close control
Keep to public paths across farmland
Use gates and stiles to cross fences, hedges and walls
Leave livestock, crops and machinery alone
Take your litter home
Help to keep all water clean
Protect wildlife, plants and trees
Take special care on country roads
Make no unnecessary noise

The most important item of equipment for the walker is footwear. You may come across quite a lot of mud even in summer so the best protection is to have a lightweight pair of boots. Most walkers get them a size too big and then wear an extra pair of thick socks to stop them rubbing. When turned down over the top of the boot they will stop small stones getting down under the feet. When you get back to the car you can take them off and change back into clean shoes. Boots are also advisable when the ground is hard and dry because the muddy gateways and tracks dry into very uneven ground and it is easy to twist an ankle in an unguarded moment.

The numbers of the Ordnance Survey maps covering the area concerned are to be found at the beginning of each walk: the Landranger series (magenta covers) at 1¼ inches to the mile, and the Pathfinder series (green covers) at 2½ inches to the mile. Many of the walks in the south of the Wye valley are to be found on the Outdoor Leisure Map No 14, which is also at 2½ inches to the mile. To have a map of the district adds considerable interest to the walk, as it is possible to identify distant objects not shown on the sketch map.

The instructions *bear right* or *left* (45°) which is half way to *turn right* or *left* (90°) and *turn back to right* or *left* (over 90°) are given to indicate a change of direction. On entering a field the direction is given assuming you stand with your back to the gate or stile, otherwise it is the deviation from the path you have been following.

*Not to scale*

# ST PIERRE'S GREAT WOOD

WALK 1

★

4 miles (6.5 km)

OS Landranger 162, Pathfinder ST 49/59

St Pierre's Great Wood is set on high ground overlooking the Severn where it is joined by the Wye. What is usually a conflict between timber farming and recreation has here been skilfully moulded together. The rotation of crops, which give variety to the eye, are seen at their best from the well laid out and maintained paths. The edges of these paths and the forest roads are full of wild flowers and shrubs which are the homes of innumerable insects and their predators, the birds. It is an excellent walk for observing natural history.

The wood is best reached from the large roundabout on the southern outskirts of Chepstow, 1 mile from junction 22 on the M4. From this roundabout take the A48 road to Caerwent and Newport. In 1 mile look for a turning on the right opposite the New Inn signposted to Shirenewton, and in a further ¼ mile fork left. The small parking area is ½ mile along this lane on the left (GR: ST 536 930).

Leave the car park by the only way into the wood and follow the forest walk through the wood passing a turning on the right. You will come back down here. This wood was once coppiced – that is the trees were cut down to ground level every so often and the young shoots used for making baskets, fish-traps and coracles. How long will it be before these trees are replaced by some in greater demand?

After you have been walking for ¼ mile turn left along a forest road. As you go along you may see a shattered snail shell. This will be where a thrush has used a large stone as an anvil to hammer the shell to get at the succulent snail within. Thirty yards after the first bend there is a sign on the left which says 'Llwybr Cyhoeddus'. Fortunately for some it also says 'Public Footpath'. Turn left and go down this very attractive path. A wood of broadleafed trees is much more user-friendly than a wood of conifers. After the hunting gate, continue ahead to a gate in the fence on the right. From this gate turn left and in 100 yards, when the ridge on the right ends, bear right up to a gate. In the next field go forward for 10 yards and then over a stile in the hedge on the left. Now turn right and keep near the hedge to a stile.

On the lane beyond turn right. Pass the farm on the left which is fast becoming a small hamlet. The lane now turns into a track with multi-species hedges on either side. At the road turn right through a gate, following a footpath sign, and walk with the old fence posts and some hawthorn bushes on the left. On approaching the wood again bear slightly right to a stile and enter the wood. In a further 100 yards turn back to the left along a forest road.

From time to time you come across areas of forest which have been cleared and replanted. In other places there are patches of young trees and in others there are tall well grown trees. The forester manages the wood in much the same way as the farmer manages the fields but, whereas the farmer harvests the crop every year, the forester has to wait up to 50 or more years. After cutting down all the trees (clear-felling), all the seeds, which have lain dormant for many years, suddenly spring into life and there is a wonderful show of flowers in summer. Gradually the trees grow and their spreading branches (the canopy) cut out the light. Conifers are especially efficient at this, creating twelve months' total blackout. Sometimes trees blow down or a forest road is made, then lo! . . . next year there is a multitude of wild flowers.

Continue along the forest road passing the sign on the right 'Rhodfa'r goedwig'. When the road goes downhill there are strands of traveller's joy intertwined with the branches, sometimes to the very top. Go round the bend at the bottom of the hill and in 100 yards start to look for a path on the right. This path goes through the undergrowth for a few yards and then enters the wood. As there is no undergrowth you will see an old, faint, rutted track going straight up the steep slope. Follow this track, avoiding any fallen trees and noting your direction. At the top cross straight over the complicated junction of old tracks. In a few yards the track goes downhill to the edge of the wood. Turn right and walk with the fence on the left. In a few yards the old track arrives at the end of a new forest road with a gate on the left. Turn right and go along the grass road.

Continue along this forest road for ¾ mile, to a major turning to the right. In a further 200 yards look for a path on the right, opposite a small clearing on the left. This path descends straight and steadily to a T junction. (Do your recognise where you are?) Turn left back to the car park.

# CHEPSTOW

## WALK 2

★

6 miles (9.5 km)

OS Landranger 162, and Outdoor Leisure 14,
Wye Valley and Forest of Dean

Chepstow is the gateway to the Wye Valley. The name given to it by the Britons was Castell Gwent and today it is still known to the Welsh by the shortened version Cas Gwent. Though the Normans called it Stiguil, the name did not stick and it soon reverted to the one given to it by the Saxons – Cheapstow or 'market town'. The castle, as we know it today, was started soon after the Norman Conquest and the town grew rapidly under its walls. Strongbow, the conqueror of Ireland, was born in the castle and later it played an important role in the Civil War. The Portwall, which was built to protect the civilian population, now cuts right through the town but originally it formed the southern limit. The nearby crossing of the Severn at Beachley, called the Old Passage, had always been a chancy business until the roadbridge was completed in 1966.

Cars can be parked in the large Portwall car park, which is at the upper end of the town, near the medieval Portwall Gate. The entrance to the car park is from the side road opposite the George Hotel. The walk starts from the doorway in the great Portwall which forms the western edge of the car park (GR: ST 535 940).

Go through a small doorway in the Portwall into a children's playground which overlooks the dry ditch round the castle. In 200 yards you come to the main B4235 road out of Chepstow to the north and west. Turn right and walk along the road for ¼ mile. As you near the top of the hill look on the right for a 'Wye Valley Walk' sign pointing to the Leisure Centre car park. Turn right and go to the far left corner of the car park. Now follow the fenced-off path below the sports field. At the end, go through the gap in the wall and turn down to the right.

This leads to a viewing point, where a bend in the Wye can be seen to have cut a wide gorge. Two million years ago the sea level was much higher than it is today and the river Wye wandered over a plain. Since then the water level has been dropping which

11

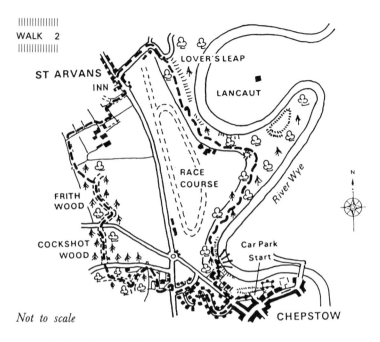

ST ARVANS

INN

LOVER'S LEAP

LANCAUT

RACE
COURSE

FRITH
WOOD

COCKSHOT
WOOD

River Wye

N

Car Park

Start

*Not to scale*

CHEPSTOW

caused the river to become more vigorous, eroding downwards very rapidly to form a valley of ever increasing depth. From time to time some of the meanders became cut off and the river, continuing to cut its way down, left these 'ox-bows', as they are called, at a higher level. One is followed on walk 8, another can be found between Ross and Kerne Bridge. Perhaps, in another million years, the loop at Tintern will have been cut off. Continue along the well walked path for the next mile, going through a yew wood. These trees were common in the Welsh marches in the Middle Ages.

After climbing up to the earthworks of a small fort, there are very good views down through the trees to the Lancaut bend. On the left was a great house called Piercefield, now in ruins, but its park is a fine setting for Chepstow race course. A short way past a small cave on the left, known as the Giant's Cave (this giant was not very fat), start to look for a track which goes up to the left. At this point the Wye Valley Walk is going down, to continue along the hillside. Bear left up a zig-zag path to the top and turn right.

Continue along the top path with periodical glimpses of the Wye far below on the right and a field on the left. In ¼ mile the path comes to 'Lover's Leap'. Keep children under complete control and anyone who has not a head for heights should pursue a route a few yards to the left, away from the edge of the precipice. Walk on out to the A466 Chepstow – Monmouth road. Turn left along the grass verge and when it ends cross the road and face the oncoming traffic. Pass the turning to Wyndcliff and in a few yards join the pavement. This takes you to St Arvans. At the road junction you may admire the circular drinking fountain, with its water-boys and dolphins, but no water. Until this century the main road from Chepstow to Monmouth came down the Devauden road, though a road up the valley through Tintern had developed since the 17th century.

Turn towards Chepstow and pass the Piercefield Inn on the right. In 100 yards, opposite a turnpike milestone set in the wall, turn right through a gate onto a concrete road, signposted Cophill 2 km. When the road bears right through a gate to a sewage works, keep straight on along the edge of the field and go through a gate. For the next ½ mile the right of way has been diverted, but not waymarked. In the next field turn left and walk with the hedge on the left as far as a fence. Here turn right and when you get as far as the gate on the left, bear right up to another gate 50 yards away. This takes you into another field so that you can go ahead next to a hedge on the left.

Continue with the hedge on the left through a number of enclosures, some of which are temporary, until you arrive in the bottom of a valley. Turn left over a stile and follow the hedge on the right. This used to be a hedged track. At the corner of the field go through a gate into Frith Wood. Walk up the main track to the forest road and turn right. Continue along and then down to the right to the road. Cross the road and keep to the main forest road beyond the barrier. In ¼ mile pass an old limekiln on the left and arrive at another road.

Cross this road and pass into the wood on the other side to go down to a track. Here turn left, parallel to the main road. The track soon curves away from the road and crosses a small stream. Now turn left along the forest road. In a short distance the track comes out onto the road. Walk along it with care. Just round the bend there is a stile on the right. In the next field bear left up to a stile next to the tall fence round the Forensic Science Laboratory and go up the narrow path to the top. In the field turn left and in a few yards go over a stile on the left so as to follow the tall fence. Keep the same direction out to the main road, which is best crossed here, and turn right.

In 100 yards turn left along Kingsmark Lane. Pass the turning to the right and in 50 yards go down a footpath between the houses. Keep ahead, to go up a flight of steps and ahead to a road. Turn right and go down through the housing estate. At the main road, almost ahead, is the children's playground through which you came at the start of the walk.

# CHEPSTOW PARK WOOD

WALK 3

★

4 miles (6.5 km)

OS Landranger 162, 171, and Outdoor Leisure 14,
Wye Valley and Forest of Dean

Chepstow Park Wood is 4 miles north west of Chepstow. It lies on
the south side of the B4293. If you are travelling from St Arvans
and the A466, the Forestry Commission car park is on the left,
almost opposite a turning to Tintern and the Cot (GR:
ST 500 985).

Walk back out of the car park across the road and between two
gateposts into New Wood. Keep straight ahead and go down a
sunken track to the enlarged end of the forest road. This is where
the foresters sort out the timber ready for dispatch. Bear slightly
left across this area and continue down the track which, for a few
yards, is not so well used. Continue past the side of the cottage
and on down the entrance track to a lane. Walk down the lane
and in 100 yards cross one of the many brooks. Before reaching
the house ahead on the left, turn left up a track, which becomes
a hollow way as it climbs the hill. This is one of the rural roads
which was not needed as a through road and was therefore not
improved for much of its length. At the top of the first rise there
is a barn on the left.

This interesting building has windows reminiscent of those in
castles, a narrow opening with a splay on the inside. Were the
builders carrying on a local building tradition? The barn is a
standard three bay with a threshing floor in the centre. The two
side bays would have been used for storage, on one side
unthreshed straw and on the other the threshed straw. The porch
has been added later; the builders did not bother to key the walls
in to the main building so sooner or later the two will drift apart.
During periods of agricultural prosperity farm buildings were built
or improved. In this case the porch was added so that at harvest
time at the end of the day one waggon would stand in the centre
of the building and another under the porch. Then in the
morning, whilst the dew was drying out in the fields, both
waggons could be unloaded. It was also useful if the weather

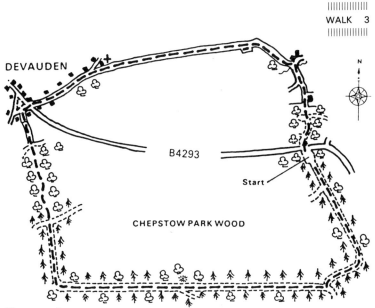

DEVAUDEN

B4293

Start

CHEPSTOW PARK WOOD

N

*Not to scale*

suddenly prevented further work in the fields.

Continue along the old road for a further ¾ mile to walk along the side of the Masons' Arms and so into the village of Devauden. Cross the road and pass the modern village hall on the left. At the end of the wire fence turn left up a wide hedged track, signposted 'Itton 2.9 km'. On reaching the wood you have a choice of a number of different paths. Choose the one immediately ahead. This narrow path climbs up the hillside between high banks and emerges onto a forest road at a junction. Walk up the forest road opposite. This eventually turns round to the left and then stretches straight ahead for just over 1 mile.

Here there is a mixture of trees along the edge. As summer progresses you will be able to find evidence of the gall wasp. There are a number of different small winged or wingless insects in this family and each one produces a different type of gall. Look under some of the oak leaves and you will find small red pills, larger orange ones and large yellow marbles. Perhaps at the end of a stalk, where there should be a small bud, there is a large swelling which looks like a small artichoke. Again on another stalk there may be a pink furry ball. These are all galls, produced by the tree to encapsulate the egg of the gall wasp.

When the forest road forks bear left and in ½ mile you will arrive back at the start.

15

# TINTERN

The development of Tintern took place in three stages. The arrival of the Cistercians in 1131 put the vale of Tintern on the map. The Cistercians had to settle for the isolated north and west because so much of south and east England was already in ecclesiastical hands. This efficient organisation obtained a large area of hill lands on which to develop its sheep production, in a district where the indigenous farmer specialised in cattle farming. With their expertise and ready markets though the parent house in Europe, the venture flourished. At the end of the 13th century they had 2,300 head of sheep. According to the Little Red Book of Bristol they had the edge over their competitors in the 14th century as they enjoyed freedom from toll 'throughout the lands of the King of England' – even though their wool was described as 'of the worst quality'. Gradually their fortunes diminished and they were suppressed along with the lesser monasteries.

The second stage started 30 years after the suppression in 1566, when William Humfres introduced German experts to Tintern and started a wire drawing works. With an abundant supply of water from the Fedw brook to provide power and a good tidal river on which to transport the finished goods, Tintern became a centre of the iron industry. It was only gradually that the economies of steam power and the rise of the South Wales valleys forced most of the forges to close during the 19th century.

The third stage began with the motor car. The beauty of the setting and the remains of the first 'boom town' attract numerous visitors who are gradually leaving their mark on the countryside.

This walk is to the top of the hill opposite the Abbey car park and then along Offa's Dyke. In some places it may be muddy from the heavy traffic of walking boots and in one place it is rather stony.

Tintern is 4 miles north of Chepstow on the A466 road. It is 8 miles south of Monmouth and well signposted from all directions. The walk starts from the car park next to the Abbey ruins (GR: SO 532 000).

16

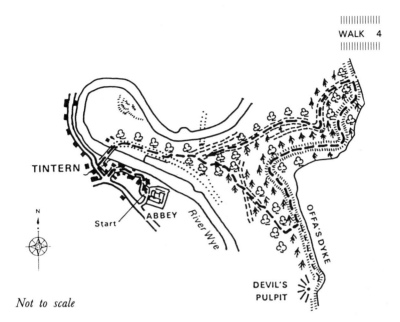

*Not to scale*

Leave the Abbey car park and go to the riverside. Turn left and follow the path. The bungalows over to the right were built on the old quay. Continue out to the main road and turn right past the shops and then look over the stone wall at the rusting water wheel. At the end of the wall turn right and cross the river. The bridge was built in 1876 to connect the Tintern wire works with the newly opened Chepstow to Monmouth railway, which ran along the other side of the river. The bridge is interesting, being made by the 'Isca Foundry Co., Newport', the same firm which made the Old Pier at Weston-super-Mare in 1867.

Go along the track, being careful not to trip over the old sleepers. Follow the yellow arrows along the main path and in 200 yards notice the stone track going steeply up the hillside. Before the railways came, much of the cross country traffic was by packhorse or on the human back. Gradients which no normal motor vehicle would ever attempt seem to have been common-place. It is no wonder that so many people did not live to an old age if they spent their time carrying heavy loads on such routes as this. Nevertheless you go up this track.

When the path levels out for a few yards there is a fork. The path to the left is to Brockweir with Tintern Old Station down to the left across the river, so fork right following the yellow arrows. In a few yards the second fork to the left is the path you will come back along. There are more yellow arrows and sometimes signposts to lead you to the top, where there is a signpost with the

17

Offa's Dyke waymark – an acorn. At this T junction, Chepstow is 9½ miles to the right, Prestatyn 265 miles to the left. The Devil's Pulpit is ½ mile to the right but if you visit it you will have to return to this point as the walk continues to the left.

The Devil's Pulpit is a small square of rock jutting out from the hillside and used by the Devil to harangue the monks. What he said is not recorded as it may have been difficult to hear his words from 1 mile up the valley. It you decide not to go to the Devil's Pulpit turn left along Offa's Dyke. This ditch and bank was the western boundary of Offa's Kingdom of Mercia towards the end of the 8th century. It was a reminder to Celtic Britain not only of the position of the boundary, but also of the presence to the east of a most powerful king.

Follow the well trodden path for nearly a mile to where it goes down to a cross track. Ahead, the Dyke goes on down to Brockweir. To the right is a gate and stile in to a field but you turn left down a wide forest road. After a while the forest road, which has been curving round the hillside to the left, suddenly turns right over the head of a valley. The ground becomes muddy and there are ferns and mosses on the left and as you come out of the bend look carefully for a narrow track down to the right. The first few yards may be overgrown with bracken, it was altered here when they made the forest road. Go down here and along the hillside until you encounter the track you followed on the way up. Retrace your steps down to the railway and so across the bridge to Tintern.

*Beech*

# TIDENHAM CHASE

## WALK 5

★

4 miles (6.5 km)

OS Landranger 162, and Outdoor Leisure 14,
Wye Valley and Forest of Dean

Tidenham Chase is a collection of woodlands connected with the large manor of Tidenham. The village of Tidenham is now only small but the parish is still large, stretching from beneath the Severn Bridge in the south almost to Tintern in the north. This walk starts on the parish boundary and explores Oakhill Wood and Little Meend. It is easy walking, though in places it may be a little muddy in wet weather.

The walk starts from a layby on the B4228 Chepstow – Coleford road, 2 miles south of St Briavels and 4½ miles north of Chepstow. From Chepstow turn left off the A38(T) ¼ mile from the river bridge. The layby is a length of old road near the top of a hill at the north end of the woods (GR: SO 565 008).

Leave the parking place at the top end and cross the road onto a wide grass verge. Follow the road (south) round the bend and in 100 yards bear right to enter Oakhill Wood. Go under the barrier, which is to stop cars driving all over the forest, and turn right onto a narrow grass path. As you go along you will notice that the pines have been interplanted with Sitka spruce. After nearly ½ mile you come to a T junction and turn right. As you go down you will see, climbing up the trees, traveller's joy – sometimes known as 'old man's beard', from its autumnal coat of greyish-white woolly plumes which form on the fruits. At the bottom turn left and continue for ½ mile, until you come to an old forest road coming up from the right. Here turn left and gradually climb to a clearing made by the foresters to assemble the tree trunks when they are clearing parts of the wood. In the right hand corner is a stile and beyond a house, but you turn left. This good forest road has on its edges many nests of wood ants, who can often be seen crossing from one side to the other.

You may notice the great mounds of bark shavings at the side of the forest road. When the forester is thinning out a plantation he has a quantity of poles which are to be sold for fencing posts.

19

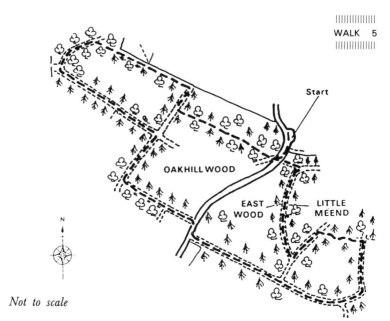

Start

OAKHILL WOOD

EAST
WOOD

LITTLE
MEEND

N

*Not to scale*

These are often treated against rot before selling and this is done
in large tanks in the woodyard. The bark must first be removed
and this is best done whilst the wood is still in the forest. A job
which used to be very laborious is now done with a mobile barking
machine. The logs are fed in at one end and side-cutters gently
rotate the log whilst stripping off the bark. This bark is shot out
to one side, so it is not difficult to tell where the work was done.

Continue for nearly ½ mile to a wide crossing of forest roads.
To the left can be seen wild rhododendrons. At this point turn
right. It will be seen that the woodland is divided into
approximately rectangular areas. A managed wood is much like an
ordinary farm, with its rectangular fields. Each area is cut down
and replanted in rotation, according to the size and type of tree
required. So the forester is always at work and there is a steady
supply of timber. In 200 yards turn left with pines on the left and
an oak wood on the right. What a difference there is here – a
dark and uninviting wood on the left and a light, pale green,
relaxing wood on the right. Walk on as far as the road and turn
right.

In 50 yards cross the road and enter East Wood. Keep straight
ahead, passing the turning to the left, to go over the rise. From
this high ground it may be possible to see the wide river Severn
as it winds its way up from the Bristol Channel. You are here
opposite Berkeley Power Station. You may, however, not be able
to see anything because of the trees, which grow at the rate of

12 inches a year. It is easy to tell the age of pines as they make a whorl of branches on the trunk each year. The total growth for each year takes place between May and July and from then on the tree is at work making next year's growth, in miniature, inside the bud. To tell the age from seed, count the whorls. Not more than 100 yards past the bend in the track, at the beginning of the mature wood, turn left on a narrow path through the trees. This will take you up to a grass forest road, where you turn left. When you reach another forest road merging in from the right, turn right. You have now walked round almost a square, so if you do not turn right you will soon be back on the way into East Wood. Having turned right the track is seen ahead to be undulating but straight.

At the bottom of the dip you can see in the trees ahead on the right an old stone wall. This means that there was once open country on one or both sides. They do not build walls in woods. Up near the wall is a spring which comes down to the little pool next to the road. It is said that this is called Heather Pool – is this significant?

Continue to where the forest road sweeps round to the right. Now turn left along a narrow path. This will bring you to the road 50 yards from the start, which is to the right.

*Durmast Oak*

# TRELLECK BEACON

## WALK 6

★

3½ miles (5.5 km)

OS Landranger 162, and Outdoor Leisure 14,
Wye Valley and Forest of Dean

Trelleck was an important stage on the Monmouth – Chepstow
road, which took the higher and dryer ground before the modern
road down the valley was made. The three standing stones and the
tumulus testify to the importance of the site to early man.

The village of Trelleck is on the B4293 about midway between
Chepstow and Monmouth. It can also be reached from Llandogo
by a somewhat steep and narrow lane. The car can be parked at
a small picnic site (GR: SO 510 053), ¾ mile east of Trelleck, on
the edge of the wood. The site looks down across the fields to the
village, from a road which runs parallel to the main street. It can
be reached from either end of the village.

From the car park go up through the picnic site and turn left on
a path. In 50 yards, before reaching the top of the hill, turn back
to the right on a narrow path. In a short distance, at the T
junction, bear right. The path to the left goes up to the beacon,
now covered with trees. In a few yards turn left along a good path
through the trees. At the cross tracks turn right down a rutted
track between beech trees. In ¼ mile, at the next cross tracks,
choose the one which maintains the same direction. This track
becomes a path and, at a meeting of a number of paths, turn
sharp left. Continue to the rough road and turn right.

Walk past the entrance to Cleddon Hall and in 20 yards look on
the left for a kissing gate in the wall. Go through this and cross
the field diagonally to the right of the pillar seen in the distance.
As you go across you will see another kissing gate in the wall just
to the right of a line of short trees. On the road beyond turn left
and pass the original entrance to Cleddon Hall. In ¼ mile go
down the first turn on the right, across the brook, which you will
see later, and round to the left of the house ahead. The road soon
narrows and comes to a cross track. This track is part of the Wye
Valley Walk – Chepstow sharp right (not the track which bears
right down the hill), to the left Hereford.

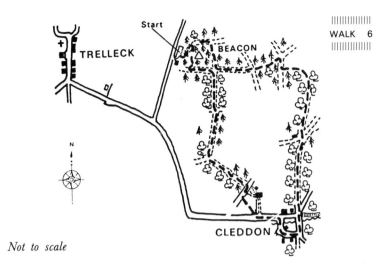

*Not to scale*

Turn left and you will soon come to the little brook again winding its way towards you on the left, but on the right it tumbles down the hillside, dropping over 300 ft in less than 150 yards. A flight of steps has been built next to the falls down to Llandogo, which are said to be longer coming up than going down! Cross the road and go up the path opposite, still following the Wye Valley Walk. This path rises steadily for ½ mile, when it forks. Here you leave the Wye Valley Walk, and go left for a few yards up to a wide forest road. Cross the road and go up the path, leaving the wooden sheds on the left, to continue climbing. The path levels out and curves round to the left to rise gently to a forest road. Now turn right and in 100 yards turn sharp left up a path which has water flowing down it in wet weather.

Cross a wide forest road and in ¼ mile you come to a cross track. (Do you recognise where you are?) Earlier you came along the track opposite and went down the beech avenue to the left. Now you turn right and soon come to a T junction when you turn left. This track curves round to the left and Trelleck Beacon is on your left. As the track starts to go down notice the path leading off to the left which you took at the beginning of the walk. Continue down the path and look through the trees on the right for the picnic area and car park.

# NEWLAND

## WALK 7

★

5 ½ miles (9 km)

OS Landranger 162, and Outdoor Leisure 14,
Wye Valley and Forest of Dean

The river Wye has not always followed exactly the same course that it does today. In its early days it meandered over a plain, making its leisurely way to the sea. Then the level of the plain gradually rose, causing the river to speed up and cut deeper into its bed. This walk follows one of the ancient meanders. It must have been much the same as the one at Sellack (Walk 25) at one time, but early in its life it cut through the neck of land at Redbrook. Since then the river has continued to cut its way deeper and deeper, so that now it is nearly 400 ft lower than its fossil meander.

Newland is 3 miles south east of Monmouth and 6 miles north west of Lydney. It lies on the B4231 about 1½ miles from Clearwell and about 2 miles from the A466 at Redbrook. Cars should be parked close to the edge of the road at the side of the churchyard, not along the main road which tends to be rather narrow. The side road has in it a fine row of almshouses, founded in 1615 and recently restored (GR: SO 553 095).

Leave the village along the main road towards Redbrook, passing the Ostrich Inn on the right. A little beyond the end of the farm buildings on the left, at the end of the village turn left at the footpath sign. From the stile bear right and cross the field towards the left hand end of the wood on the hill ¼ mile away. As you go over the field you will see a gate in the angle of the hedge. Bear left and go through the gate and up the next field near the hedge on the left. Pass a gate on the left and at the top of the ridge go over a fence on the left and walk with the hedge now on the right. Continue through three more fields. In the second field there is a spring a short way up the field but a boarded walk-way takes you over the wet ground. Notice the marker stones on the boundary on the right, bearing various farmers' initials. They may date back to pre-enclosure days when they marked the plots on the open common land put up for hay making in summer. Was there a settlement beyond the fence on the right?

24

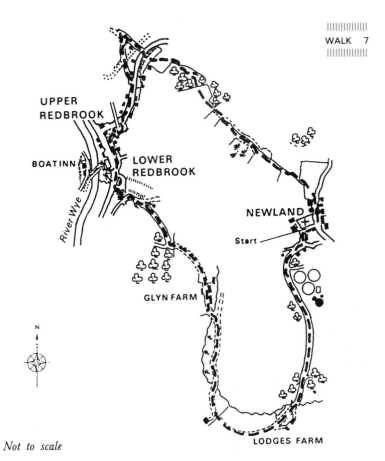

UPPER
REDBROOK

BOAT INN

LOWER
REDBROOK

River Wye

NEWLAND

Start

GLYN FARM

N

Not to scale

LODGES FARM

In the third field, go over the stile in the far corner. Now turn left to walk next to a fence. At the end of the fence go over a stile. Keep straight ahead, with the wood on the right, and when the wood ends bear slightly right to a point in the hedge 30 yards to the left of an electricity pole. Go down through the bushes to a stile and follow the path on through the wood. At the bottom of the wood there is a stile into a field. Turn left just outside the wood and when the wood ends, continue across the field aiming a little to the left of the white house seen across the valley. From a stile go down to cross the stream by the footbridge and so up onto the road – but take care, children should be under complete control.

To avoid walking down the narrow winding road to the left, go over the road and up a steep track, and on reaching the top turn back down another track. In 100 yards go over a cross track. This was once the railway line between Coleford and Monmouth. It began life as a tramroad and was turned into a railway by the GWR. Continue down the track and as you go down there is a good view over to the left of the remains of one of the Forest of Dean industrial estates. It started with a furnace in the 17th century, followed by a stamping mill and foundry, all using vast quantities of charcoal and water. On reaching the road continue, facing the oncoming traffic. The bridge with the sloping top was where a tramway from Lower Redbrook tinplate works went up to the GWR forest railway. Turn left just before reaching the bridge and follow the track, the old tramway route, round behind the houses. There are signs of past industrial activity all around. Down to the right, at the bottom of the hill, there was the large 17th century Upper Copper Works, which flourished from 1690 to 1730. The ore was brought from Cornwall to Chepstow and then up to the Wye, providing a return load for the otherwise empty boats. The building was later enlarged for a tinplate works which spread out to where the garage now stands. At the main road turn left past the Wye Valley Petrol Station and Café. Continue along the main road.

Those who wish to visit the Boat Inn should turn right to go through the car park, next to the sports field, and follow the path over the river bridge, returning the same way.

Turn left at the second turning and in a few yards turn right up a long flight of steps, waymarked 'Offa's Dyke Path'. Filling the valley on the left was the 17th century Lower Copper Works, later a tinplate works and more recently a waste paper store. At the top of the steps turn left along the road, leaving the Offa's Dyke Path to go on ahead. Go to the end of the road where one track forks left down to Glyn Farm Riding Stables, another going to a cottage and a third bearing right and gradually climbing. Bear right and in ¼ mile, at the hairpin bend, turn left. On the right is the Highbury Nature Reserve. Go down the track and walk through Glyn Farm. The track now goes over the brook and continues up the valley. In ¼ mile the track crosses back over the brook. In a further ¼ mile the track turns right up to a small stone house. Here go straight ahead along a grass track which curves round the valley to pass below Lodges Farm and on to the road to the farm. Turn left and again cross the brook on an interesting stone bridge – they don't build them like that any more. Keep ahead for another ¾ mile and at the beginning of Newland turn left uphill. At the top of the hill turn right back to the car.

# PARKEND

## WALK 8

★

4 miles (6.5 km)

OS Landranger 162, and Outdoor Leisure 14,
Wye Valley and Forest of Dean

Parkend is where the B4234 crosses the Blakeney – Coleford road, 1 mile south of Cannop. The village is formed round a large triangle, along the south end of which once ran a railway. Cars may be parked on the grass verge, now planted with trees but at one time the loading area for railway trucks (GR: SO 615 079).

To start the walk go past the Fountains Inn to the crossroads and turn right. Here is the end of the only railway line left in Dean. Until 1977 it was the headquarters of the Dean Forest Railway Preservation Society, but then the society moved 3 miles down the Lydney road to a larger site. Turn left across the railway by the footbridge and go up the hill past the cottages to the church. Walk on into the forest and go down to a large forest road junction. There is now the choice of three forest roads and one smaller track. Go straight ahead up this track, which has been enlarged at the beginning by cutting away the high banks. Until recently the forester used horses to pull out the timber. Today the larger motorised vehicles need both wider and firmer surfaces on which to operate. This is one of the old horse tracks, as well as being an old road between Parkend and Yorkley. On the right are the remains of an old coppiced chestnut wood.

Cross straight over the next forest road. Keep children and dogs on the track here as there are old mine shafts in the woods and they are dangerous. Continue straight ahead to go down past a free miners' mine, abandoned a few years ago. To be a free miner, it is necessary to be 'born within the Hundred of St Briavels, the son of a Free Miner, and to be resident therein. Also to have worked a year and a day in an iron mine, coal work or stone quarry of some other Free Miner'. This gale, as the sloping shaft is called, went deep into the hill and had to be ventilated with an air compressor which stood outside.

Just past here there is a grass track which used to be a railway line. Turn left and walk along the embankment until the path

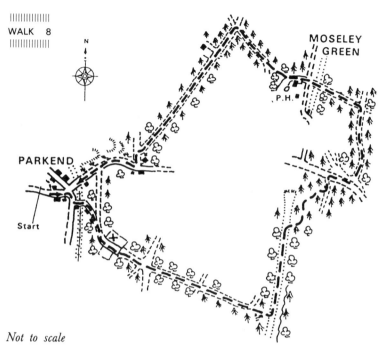

WALK 8

MOSELEY GREEN

N

PARKEND

Start

P.H.

*Not to scale*

turns right on to a ridge and continues, to emerge onto a forest road. Turn left and on reaching the road, cross and turn right. In 100 yards turn left along a wide forest road. In ¼ mile, at the metal electricity pole, turn left and keep straight ahead. At the far end of the wood cross the old railway track, which has come through the hill from where you left it on the way up. Go out to the road and go up the track opposite, which goes to the Rising Sun Inn. At the top of the track keep straight ahead up the grass bank and in a few yards, opposite the end of the building on the left, turn right. Keep this direction for ¼ mile to a well used gravel road. Turn back to the left. This is Church Hill, because it was owned by the church. The area is now known as Churchill Inclosure. In years to come will something here become connected with the 1939-45 war? This is the stuff that legends are made from. Soon the road turns right to Churchill Lodge but keep straight ahead along a grass track.

Continue straight ahead to the road. On the left are the remains of one of the forest giants. It was called the School Oak from the school on the other side of the road. Turn right and go down the road. At the bottom of the hill go straight over the crossroads, past the tearooms on the left, back to the car.

# BLACKPOOL BRIDGE

4 5 Hilly.

★

4 miles (6.5 km)

OS Landranger 162, and Outdoor Leisure 14,
Wye Valley and Forest of Dean

During the Roman occupation and probably for many years before
that, the Dean provided iron for the armies and farmers of south
and west Britain. The development of the heavy iron-clad plough
led to an increased demand for iron. Therefore roads had to be
upgraded to take the increased traffic. A short length of early
road, built to Roman specifications, has been exposed and
maintained near Blackpool Bridge.

The Forestry Commission has provided many parking and
picnic sites in the forest. Wench Ford is a good example of how
this can be done without spoiling the environment. The car park
is situated off the B4431, one mile north west of Blakeney on the
road to Parkend and Coleford. It can also be reached from the
north by turning off the B4227 on a sharp bend south of
Cinderford. The road through the forest is signposted to Blackpool
Bridge and starts by going over a cattle grid.

There are two entrances to the car park. Use the northern one
at Blackpool Bridge, next to the old railway bridge at the junction
of the Cinderford road with the B4431. If you can, park near this
end, as the walk comes back to this part of the car park (GR:
SO 652 085).

Walk down the gravel road to the toilet block. The whole length
of this park is set out on the bed of the ill-fated Forest of Dean
Central Railway which ran from the New Fancy Colliery down to
Awre Junction east of Blakeney. It was never completed at the
northern end (see Walk 10). Go up behind the toilet block to a
good track and turn right. Follow this track, which was once the
road down the valley, up to a forest road. Turn right downhill and
at the bend keep straight ahead, to go uphill. At the top of the rise
keep straight ahead. When the wood ends go out onto a road and
turn right downhill and round the bend. When the railings on the
right end, turn back to the right downhill, past the Rudge on the
right and row of hawthorns on the left. This path will take you

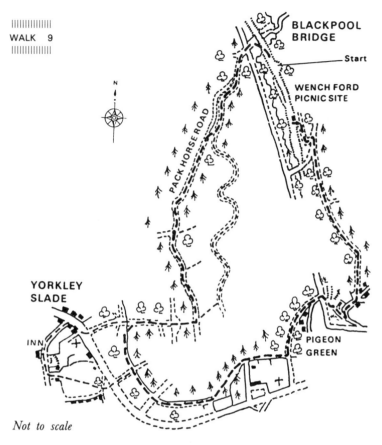

**BLACKPOOL BRIDGE**

Start

**WENCH FORD PICNIC SITE**

PACK HORSE ROAD

N

**YORKLEY SLADE**

INN

**PIGEON GREEN**

*Not to scale*

down to the main road. Bear right along the grass verge for 50 yards and cross the road to walk up a narrow lane. Twenty yards up the lane fork right along a grass track which goes along the back of the houses at Pigeon Green.

Continue climbing up the hill until you come to a gate at the top. Do not go through but turn right along a path which follows the wall on the left. In 200 yards, when the boundary turns left, go ahead along a cleared path through the spruce wood. The path starts by bearing left and in ¼ mile goes down to a track along the edge of the wood. Cross a forest road and continue to the second forest road. Here those who need refreshment leave the grass track and turn left, and miss the next paragraph.

Those wishing to continue, keep to the track along the edge of the wood, now on the other side of the fence, until it bears right and arrives at a grass path where it enters the wood. Turn right along this and miss the next paragraph.

30

Follow the gravel track out to the main road, cross with care and bear right across a sports field to go between houses out to a lane. Turn right to The Nags Head. To return to the walk, go up the lane and at the main road turn right. When the woodland begins on the left, turn left and go to a gate which leads to a grass track through the forest. Continue along this track.

At the cross tracks go straight over and on down to a very wide forest road. Go straight over again and down the grass path to an intersection. To the right the path goes gently downhill and to the left it goes along the hillside. Turn left. This is the Roman road, not a military straight highway but a packhorse and packman road, and one of the few public rights of way in the forest. If the path is affected by forestry work a detour may be made to the right down any of the paths to a wide forest road where you turn left. This road winds its way roughly parallel to the path above. They both come together for the last ½ mile before arriving at the main road. Cross this with care and go along the road opposite.

To examine the Roman road pass under the disused railway bridge. Return under the bridge and turn into Wench Ford.

*Norway Spruce*

# CANNOP PONDS  4/5

WALK 10

★

6½ miles (10.5 km)

OS Landranger 162, and Outdoor Leisure 14,
Wye Valley and Forest of Dean

This walk is through the heart of the Forest of Dean. It includes
three of the best known 'honeypots' and is full of interest. The
start is from the picnic site between two ponds and is reached from
the B4226, 200 yards on the Cinderford side of the crossroads at
Cannop. Look for the Forestry Commission signboard at the
bottom of the hill below Speech House and drive along the asphalt
track, noting the many 'sleeping policemen', to the far end of the
first lake. Park under the trees in the bays provided (GR:
SO 610 108). The two lakes were manmade in the early 19th
century to store water for the iron works at Parkend, just over a
mile down the valley.

At the beginning of the walk there is a choice of two routes. One
goes opposite the car park through the grass picnic area and to the
left to wind its way along the edge of the second lake. The other
goes along a continuation of the road with the 'sleeping
policemen'. If you follow this route you will see that you are on
old railway track – only abandoned about 1965. Both routes
come together at the end of the second lake. Here a short digres-
sion to the right across the dam brings you to the Forest of Dean
stone firm's yard.

It is here that stone from a quarry, high up on the other side
of the valley, is cut to various sizes. The stone is Pennant
sandstone, known as 'forest marble', and has three colours,
yellow-brown when there is limonite present, grey when carbon-
aceous material is mixed with the sand grains, and blue when
there is a variation of the other two or iron sulphide is present. It
is highly valued for building and was used for University College
of Wales, Aberystwyth, University College, London, the Law
Courts, London, and many other fine buildings. In the quarry it
is possible to find large casts of tree trunks (stigilleria), some 280
million years old. One fine example, about four ft high, is propped
up on the right just inside the yard.

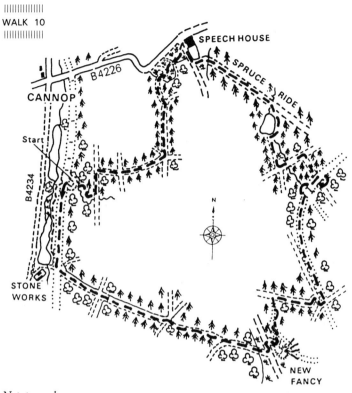

*Not to scale*

Return across the dam and go straight over the old railway. Do not follow the yellow or red arrows which go to the left into a plantation but bear right following a grass track just outside the plantation, with an old oak wood on the right. In ¼ mile go straight over the cross track and then over a stile. Continue up the hill. At the junction of roads and tracks go straight ahead up a narrow path. In ¼ mile join a forest road and follow it to the main road. Turn left along the grass verge, taking great care, as traffic tends to speed along this stretch.

In 200 yards cross the road and enter New Fancy car park. All around are the waste tips of an old coal mine which have lately been landscaped. On the right is a heap with a view. It is well worth the climb up the path. Returning to the car park go towards the picnic place, passing the toilets hidden behind a bank on your right. Go down to an old railway track and turn left. The stone wall on the left is where the coal was fed into railway trucks. At the foot of the wall a length of track has been left. It was in use until 1944 when the colliery was closed. From the stile in the

33

corner turn left and follow the grass path. As you go along it you will see plenty of evidence of the old railway lines. This was the old shunting yard, on a slight gradient so that the loaded trucks could be sorted without the use of an engine. The track tends to become waterlogged but it is quite easy to follow the path to the right, part of a nature walk.

On reaching the T junction turn right down a very pleasant grass ride, bordered with a great variety of young trees. The sallow or goat willow predominates. This is a spring willow, that is one which flowers before the leaves come. (The summer willows, such as the crack willow, which is often pollarded and found along the margins of streams, flower late.) There are also a lot of silver birch and if you look carefully you can find oak, mountain ash, holly, hazel, hawthorn, ash and sycamore.

At the end of the ride you come out on to a forest road. Turn right and in 20 yards, at the junction where there is a lime tree on the corner, turn left. In 20 yards you are standing on another old railway track. Turn left along the grassed-over track. You are now walking along the Severn and Wye Railway Company's Mineral Loop line. This was opened in 1872 and was in use for 81 years. It was 7 miles long and served many collieries in this part of the forest. All the plants growing on the track have seeded themselves and grown in less than 30 years. It does not take long for nature to cover over the efforts of man. How many flowers can you recognise? Here are some: birds-eye speedwell, wood spurge, horsetail, vetch, clover, stitchwort, heather and the bush guelder rose. There are also clumps of gorse, some of which are sure to be showing some flower whatever the time of year – giving rise to a very sensible old country saying, 'When gorse is in bloom, 'tis kissing time'.

Keep to the old railway track until the path suddenly dives down the embankment to the left. This was where an extension of the Central Railway was to pass under the Mineral Loop. It was never completed. Climb back on to the track. The next bridge was built over a forest ride. Go to the far end of the parapet on the right and down the steps to the ride. Turn right under the bridge. At the roadway in 200 yards turn left. In 100 yards, at the junction, turn right along a grass track. You can often see dragon-flies along here in summer. As you rise up the bank ahead you suddenly find Speech House lake in front. This was built by the Forestry Commission in 1975 as a conservation lake for wildlife. Pass either side to the other end. Continue a little further and you will come out onto a wide forest road. This is called Spruce Ride, from its fine avenue set out at the beginning of this century. Turn left along the avenue. As you get to the top of the first rise look back and you get a fine view of Staple Edge Hill. Continue through the car park out to the main road. It is the same road you crossed at New Fancy, so you may find people speeding here also. Turn right along the grass verge.

At the crossroads is Speech House. As a royal forest the Forest of Dean had officers to administer it. All that remains now are the Verderers, those responsible for 'all growing and living things', the vert and the venison. The Court of Verderers, often called 'The Court of Speech', was transferred to a new house during the reign of Charles II, and it soon became known as Speech House. The Court still sits four times a year, as it did in the time of King Canute, but there is now little or nothing for it to do.

From Speech House cross the triangle of grass at the road junction and go down a grass path which starts in front of the lower 'give way' sign. Now follow the yellow arrows. The trees here are the oldest in the forest. The holly trees are thought to date from the early 17th century, and the oaks from the last years of that century. They and the beech are long past their prime and have been dying for many years.

Cross over a narrow track and go down with a fence on the left to a forest track, where you turn left to go into Russell's Inclosure. In ¼ mile, at a T junction, turn right. In a further ¼ mile, at the junction of five ways, bear right. This track soon starts to go downhill, crossing a wide forest road and arriving at a T junction. Turn left and in 200 yards, in a hollow with a stream crossing underground, turn right over a stile. Ignore any arrows pointing elsewhere. This path winds its way through the wood with the car park at the other end. As you go along through the oak wood, if you look carefully, you can see other outcrops of coal in the banks of the stream. Some of these have been worked by the free miners. After winding through the trees you come out at the picnic site where you started.

As you drive back to the main road look on the left and you will see where a branch line went off in a gentle curve. It served the wood distillation works where they produced charcoal for gunpowder, lamp black, naphtha and many other products. It was on the level ground near the crossroads. Opposite the entrance to the roadway you are on, there is a low wall which is all that is left of a 17th century furnace.

# STAUNTON

WALK 11

★

5½ miles (9 km)

OS Landranger 162, and Outdoor Leisure 14,
Wye Valley and Forest of Dean

The village of Staunton is set high on the rim of the Forest of
Dean, on the A4136 between Monmouth and Coleford. The walk
is through the forest and visits one of the well-known viewpoints.
   The walk starts from a large layby off the main road, ½ mile
out of Staunton on the way to Coleford (GR: SO 557 123).

Leave the layby and walk along the road towards Staunton. Just
before reaching the end of the woods, turn left onto a forest road,
which soon curves left and comes back parallel to the road. Keep
straight ahead at the first junction. You will come down the forest
road on the right at the end of the walk. In ¼ mile turn right at
the cross track. Keep the same direction on reaching the wide
gravel road and in 100 yards, opposite an old track coming in on
the left, look for a narrow path on the right. Go up here and
round the edge of the wood, with the quarry on the left, to a point
100 yards along the top edge of the wood. Here the path turns
right into the wood and continues as a hard track.
   At the top of the hill go to the left along a wide forest road. In
50 yards bear right down a pleasant grass path. Go straight over
the cross tracks in 200 yards and, soon after, the path turns round
to the right. In a few yards the track forks. Take the right hand
path which curves back round the hillside and goes down to a
larger track. Here turn right and walk down to the lane.
   Keep the same direction along the lane for 50 yards and then
turn back on the lower lane. In ¼ mile there is an entrance to the
forest on the right. Go in here and take the lower forest road on
the left, which goes down the valley. In a further ¼ mile you will
start to curve round to the right. Down to the left, now hidden by
bushes, once stood one of the earliest furnaces for smelting iron.
It used the new-fangled water power, developed in the early 17th
century. Curving round, just above where the furnace stood is the
embankment of a railway which was closed down during the Great
War after it had been working for 100 years. It started as the

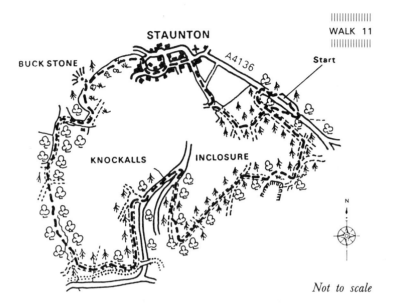

STAUNTON

BUCK STONE

A4136

Start

KNOCKALLS INCLOSURE

N

*Not to scale*

Monmouth Tramroad. The track was made up of short L shaped plates and the wheels of the horse-drawn trucks had no flanges. It was not until 1883 that it was converted into a standard gauge railway, much to the satisfaction of the people of Coleford at the eastern end of the line, who are said to have celebrated the event with great gusto.

The path now goes along the side of the valley for ¼ mile following the line of the railway, which is down on the left. Soon after a well used cross path the track makes a sharp bend round a valley on the left. Here bear right up a grass path which used to be a much wider road. In 50 yards keep straight ahead, climbing steadily.

As you go up, there are signs of small animals having their own cross tracks here. Tracks of fox, badger and deer can all be found, especially if the ground is soft. The badger is a nocturnal animal, so you will not see one going about its business. They do not like people walking about the entrance to their homes. So if you come across a badger set, respect their feelings and do not go too close. The deer is elusive. It will have heard or smelt you coming along before you arrive and will have moved off. The fox, too, is mainly nocturnal but may be seen early and late in the day in winter. If we do not see these animals we know where they have been by their footprints, their droppings and other signs left behind. If you know what to look for, places like this show how busy the forest is when we humans are not about.

Continue up to a grass forest road which bends to the right.

Cross straight over and, keeping the same direction, go on climbing. Eventually you will cross a grassed over forest road and the path will become less steep. When the path merges with a path coming up from the left walk next to the hedge on the left. The path turns into a rutted track which you follow up to the right. After passing between stone walls the track emerges onto the end of a lane, with the Adventure Centre on the right.

Cross the road and go up through the bracken, following the direction of the yellow arrow on the electricity pole. This will take you up to the Buck Stone. This used to be a rocking stone. In 1885 some touring actors came up from Monmouth and pushed too hard. It rolled down towards the road below! With unusual magnanimity the Crown brought it back and cemented it in position.

Away to your right as you climbed the last slope, you could see the village of Staunton through which you will go later. The name Staunton comes from the Anglo-Saxon stan: a stone or rock. And where better to see rocks than near Staunton? They range from the small white pebbles in the quartz conglomerate or pudding stone, to the mysterious standing stones, one of which you pass near the end of the walk. The most notable are the Longstone and the Suck Stone visited on Walk 14. To early man stones must have played an important part in life. Those that have survived the last 4,000 years of agricultural activity are but the residue of a complicated network of trackways, mounds, camps and many other so far unexplained physical features.

From the view point at the Ordnance Survey pillar walk along next to the wall on the left. This path winds its way down to a lane on the edge of Staunton. Turn left and go down to the main road. Turn right and just past the White Horse Inn, turn right and go down through the village. At the bottom turn left and walk up the street to the old cross opposite the church and turn right. The cottages here were once almshouses. Go down this ancient walled track to Highmeadow. The field on the left is thought to be the site of a windmill, and the field on the right the site of the manor house, both long since gone.

Continue up the hill keeping the same direction to the wood. Follow the wide path and where the path forks turn sharp left on to a narrower path which may be shown by a yellow arrow. This path joins a wide forest road and goes down to a T junction. Keep the same direction across this junction and go along a narrow path which eventually comes out to the main road. On the other side of the road is the Longstone, standing on the grass verge. This stone was erected in prehistoric times and its purpose is unknown. Turn left along the pavement and the car is 200 yards ahead.

# MONMOUTH

7 miles (11 km)

OS Landranger 162, and Outdoor Leisure 14,
Wye Valley and Forest of Dean

This walk starts out along the banks of the Wye and returns over
the hill from which there are fine views over Monmouth and into
the mountains of Wales.

Monmouth derives its name from its position at the mouth of
the river Monnow which rises in the Brecon Beacons and ends
when it runs into the Wye. Surrounded on three sides by rivers,
Monmouth lends itself to being a fortified town. There was a
river-crossing here in Roman times and probably before that. The
town grew when the castle was built and some degree of security
was established. Harry of Monmouth, who later became Henry V
was born here. By the Act of Union of 1536 Wales was incor-
porated into England. The March, a district stretching from
Glamorgan to Flint and including parts of Herefordshire and
Shropshire, was divided up into five shires, one of which was
Monmouthshire. This ended two and a half centuries of admini-
strative chaos. Today the county is called Gwent and the
administration has moved further west to Cwmbran. An excellent
local guide book will provide background information on the town
and its surrounding district.

Cars can be parked at various points in the town. The walk
starts from the car park near the market, off Bridge Street (GR:
SO 505 125). This park is signposted a few yards from the famous
13th century Monnow Bridge and is next to a sports ground.

The walk starts from the back of the newly furbished sheep
market, to go along a track between the river Monnow and the
back of the sports pavilion. Climb up the steps, cross the river and
go down the other side. Now go under the bridge and come out
along Beech Road. As you go along you can look down into the
abandoned Monmouth (Troy) station – now ripe for
development. Continue along the main road and at the sharp bend
turn left down a lane. The house on the corner was once a toll
house. Walk along the lane past Troy House, through the farm-

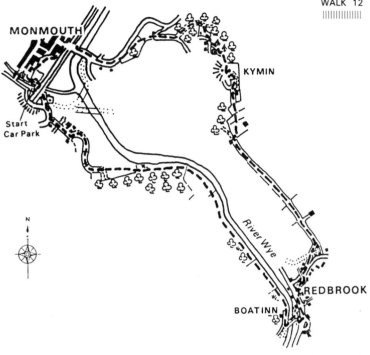

*Not to scale*

yard and then follow the yellow arrows which point sharp left to a farm track. Follow the track along the hillside for just over ¼ mile. On reaching a sloping field go straight ahead to the far left hand end of the wood on the right. Here there is a stile and a track through the wood, just above the river. At the end of the wood continue next to the river for 1½ miles. Dragonflies are numerous here. The bright blue one with the blue band across its wings is a damselfly. They do nothing but good, for most of their diet consists of mosquitoes and other small insects.

At the Boat Inn there are waterfalls at the back of the garden. The cliffs are a part of the old red sandstone block that stretches away to the west. A few yards past the inn, turn left onto the metal bridge and cross the river, and then turn right out to the main A466 road at Redbrook. Turn left along the road and walk past the Wye Valley Petrol Station and Café. In 200 yards, at the Bush Inn, turn right along the road to Coleford.

At the back of the Bush Inn there is an overgrown wall in the bank, a few yards from the road. This is all that remains of one of the side walls of the very large 17th century Upper Redbrook

Copper Works. At one time it stretched across the present main road as far as the garage you have just passed (see Walk 7).

Go under the bridge with the steeply inclined top which once carried a tramway and keep to the right hand side of the road, facing the oncoming traffic. In a few yards pass a stone building on the right which must have once used waterpower because just beyond it, over the wall, can be seen the stonework remains of a water system which channelled the stream into the building. In 200 yards fork left, leaving the road, to walk up a track at the back of a house. It is signposted 'Monmouth 3'. Follow the track up the hillside always keeping ahead at any branch tracks. Passing the last cottage on the right called Sunny Bank, bear left, keeping to the track and following the Offa's Dyke signs. Continue for ½ mile, passing an old stone barn on the left. A few yards further on go over a stile on the right into a field and turn left. Go up the field to the stile marked with a clear 'Offa's Dyke' waymark. Keep to this path up to the National Trust car park at Kymin. Bear right across the car park.

The first building you come to is the Naval Temple which was erected in 1800 to perpetuate the memory of 16 distinguished admirals whose names are displayed round the walls. The second building, 100 yards further on, was erected in 1794 as a summer house for 'the first gentlemen in Monmouth'. This building, now called the Round House, was where Nelson was entertained to breakfast on the occasion of his visit to Monmouth.

Walk on under the trees and at the wooden signpost turn left down the steps. As you go down keep a lookout for a sign directing you down the right hand side of a garden fence and through a wood. On reaching the lane turn right and then left down the lane. Almost immediately turn right over a stile to go down the field, following the waymarks. In the middle of the field keep ahead and then bear round to the right to a stile in the corner of the field. At the hollow way beyond, turn left down to a road. This is the way up for cars to the park at Kymin. Go straight ahead and in 300 yards, at the sharp right hand bend, go straight ahead through a metal gate.

Keep the same direction to another metal gate into a wood. Here there is a wide path down to the main road. It is best to cross the road before reaching the bend. In 200 yards you can see a woodyard down on the right. This was the site of the other station at Monmouth (May Hill) which was quite extensive. Cross the bridge to the traffic lights and turn right down to the subway. This will take you to the opposite side of the A40. Cross over the side road which leads to the town centre and walk by the side of the school wall, with the A40 on the left. This will take you to a park and if you walk through the avenue of trees you will come to the back of the car park where the walk started.

# SPECULATION

## WALK 13

★

5 miles (8 km)

OS Landranger 162, and Outdoor Leisure 14,
Wye Valley and Forest of Dean

The walk starts from the Forestry Commission car park set in the forest off the B4234, Ross on Wye – Lydney road. It is almost 3 miles south of Lower Lydbrook and 6 miles north of Lydney. The entrance is clearly signposted on the main road (GR: SO 613 136).

Speculation is the name of the mine which used to cover all the ground near the car park. The open space is all that is left of the huge tip after being roughly levelled.

Leave the car park along a path at the top of the open space and walk along the old railway to the right. Continue round the bend and then keep straight ahead. Just before forking right to enter the wood, look on the ground. Here was a level crossing, of which some of the timbers are still in place and a few rail chairs can be seen. In 300 yards you are at Serridge Junction. A platform was built here for the use of the keeper. In 1612 James I privatised some ironworks he owned in the Dean. With some of the proceeds he built keepers' lodges in the forest. One of these is at the top of the hill. Walk on along the old railway.

In ¼ mile you will begin to see a steep hillside up to the left. This is the beginning of an enormous waste tip which changed the shape of the hill. High up on the hill was the Trafalgar Colliery, one of the largest in the Dean in the late 19th century. As you go along notice the retaining wall on the left on either side of the bridge. This was built in 1904 after a landslip, when the waste tip blocked the railway. In the clearing, on the left beyond the bridge, was where the coal was loaded on to wagons for dispatch down to Lydney or up into Herefordshire and at the top of the hill was the mine. A little to the left of the mine was a shed where the owner of the mine, Frank (later Sir Frances) Brain experimented with the newly discovered electricity. He invented a method of firing explosives and marketed it under the name of The Electric Blasting Apparatus Co. Later he was associated with the use of electric light on the Severn Railway Bridge in 1897.

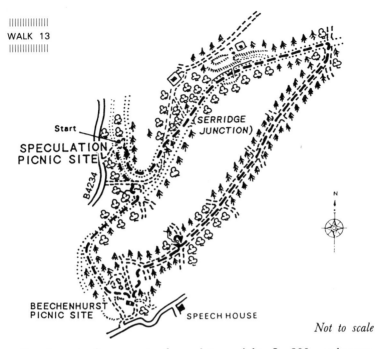

Not to scale

Continue to the cross tracks and turn right. In 200 yards turn right and follow this forest road for 1½ miles to a cross track with a small pool on the right. In a further few yards turn right and look at two of the exhibits on the Sculpture Trail. Return to the track you were on and continue up the rise to 'The Chair'. From here go down to the new Forestry Commission cafe, shop and toilets. Here it is possible to obtain hot or cold snacks at all times except Christmas Day. The picnic and play area is another flattened colliery tip. This mine was first called Rose in Hand and later Speech House Hill or Great Western.

Walk on down the car park to the exit road and turn right. This incline was the route from the colliery for first the tramroad and later the railway. At the bottom of the incline was the Wimberry Junction. Walk on round the bend and in ½ mile, at the cross tracks, turn left down to the piece of sculpture. Follow the trail to the next exhibit, some boats, to rise up to a well used track and turn left. Those following the Sculpture Trail will be turning right. In a few yards fork right along a grass track. This is the old tramroad between Serridge Junction and the Lydbrook Incline (see Walk 15). Many an old horse has trodden this way, doing the journey to Lower Lydbrook and back in 2 hours. The car park is 5 minutes along this track.

# BIBLINS

WALK 14

6 miles (9.5 km)

OS Landranger 162, and Outdoor Leisure 14,
Wye Valley and
Forest of Dean

Biblins car park has been cut in the hillside, deep in the woods,
¼ mile west of the B4432 road between Symonds Yat East and
Christchurch (GR: SO 566 137). It is signposted with a Forestry
Commission notice board at the entrance to a gravel track, 1 mile
south of Yat Rock and ½ mile north of Ready Penny car park,
which is on the outskirts of Christchurch.

Leave the car park by the lower left hand corner, cross the forest
road and go down a well-worn path. This is part of a Forest Trail
which started at the car park. As the track begins to rise the Trail
turns left, but you continue ahead up to a cross track, with a wide
forest road in front. Go along this forest road and at the first right
hand bend bear left up a rutted grass track. On reaching the
macadam road turn left and in 100 yards you come to a
T junction. Here turn right past two cottages towards the entrance
to Bracelands Camp. Just before reaching the entrance bear left
and go along a stone track. In 100 yards at a cross path, opposite
a pedestrian entrance to the camp site turn left down an old forest
road.

At the cross tracks in the valley go straight across, over a little
stream, and start a steady climb of 250 ft up to Staunton church.
When you reach the main road at Staunton, rest for a moment
and admire the old barn across the road. The small opening high
up the gable end, which in this case is triangular, was put there
to allow owls to get in and out when the barn was full of
unthrashed corn. Owls were very welcome, particularly before cats
became so plentiful, as they kept the mouse and bird population
down. Cross the road with care and keep to the left of the stump
of the old village cross. You are going along what used to be the
only road through the village. What is now the main road sweeps
round past the churchyard. About 150 years ago it was 'The Great
Staunton Bypass' – built by the Turnpike Trust to avoid the

*Not to scale*

narrow streets of the village. How the shopkeepers and innkeepers must have complained. But today the narrow street is best, so go on past the old school, which is on the right. Where did they get the three wonderful stone lintels for the porch? A little further down is a well-proportioned house which has a flight of stone steps on one side leading up to a barn. This is a reminder that much of the land round Staunton, which is now woodland, was once farmland. This was one of the few rural villages in western Gloucestershire. Continue as far as the post office, which used to be an inn, and bear right. At the main road, turn left past the White Horse Inn.

Continue along the main road towards Monmouth for 200 yards. Opposite the road sign for a sharp left hand bend, look for a narrow opening between a house and a wall, marked with a yellow arrow. Go along this path and down past St John the Baptist's Well. At the next fork in the path bear left downhill. When the steps end and one path goes to the left, keep straight ahead down to a forest road. Turn right and continue for nearly a mile until the Suck Stone can be seen up on the right.

This huge lump of rock is said to be the largest boulder in Britain. At some time, it broke off the cliff above. Looking up you will see the line of the hard rock high above the forest road you have just come along. These rocks dip down away from you at

45

about 40° and so you are looking at the underside of the layer. The rock of the hillside on which you are standing is of a clay formation and is much softer, so it wears away leaving the hard rock unsupported. This eventually fractures and great lumps roll down the hillside. Fortunately for you it does not happen very often.

Keep to the forest road past the Suck Stone leaving the yellow arrows to go up the hillside. In ¼ mile the track forks. Follow the main track to the left down the hill. On reaching another track at a bend turn right and continue to bear right until you are on an old railway. If you look ahead you can sometimes see the marks where the sleepers used to be. At the clearing by an old quarry wall there was a small siding for filling the trucks with stone. This was Hardrock Quarry. Continue along the old Ross-Monmouth railway track, said in its day to be the most beautiful line in England. In ¾ mile there is a footbridge over the river. It is an interesting experience to cross the bridge and there are some fine views of the river and the surrounding cliffs from the advantage of height.

Return to the walk upstream. In ¼ mile, at the beginning of the second valley on the right, stop and prepare to walk up the long hill back to the car. This part of the wood is called The Slaughter, not a name commemorating some terrible battle but a corruption of 'slough' – a wet place. Turn right as directed by the signpost to Christchurch and go up the wide stone track, with the deeply cut stream-bed on the left. Look for the white marker posts on the left as you go up, if you see them you are in the correct valley! About halfway up the white markers go off to the right to Bracelands. Keep to the main track. You will eventually come up to the side of the car park.

# EDGE END

## WALK 15

★

7 miles (11 km)

OS Landranger 162, and Outdoor Leisure 14,
Wye Valley and Forest of Dean

This walk starts high on the rim of the forest and goes down to the Wye. The return through the woods involves climbing about 1,000 ft, though the gradients are gentle and in some cases steps are provided.

Edge End Forestry Commission car park and picnic site (GR: SO 596 140) is off the A4136 Monmouth – Gloucester road, 2 miles north of Coleford. The entrance has only a small notice on the road, which says 'Car Park and Bed and Breakfast'. There is a Forestry Commission notice on either side some way along the main road.

The view from the car park is across the valley to English Bicknor.

Stand at the highest point in the car park with your back to the view and go along the wide gravel track. In 50 yards look carefully at the trees on the left for a yellow arrow. There are a number of these arrows painted on the trees, so follow them for 1½ miles. At the end of the wood cross the road and continue with a bank on the left as far as a track. From here the view is to Hay Bluff and the Black Mountains. Walk along the track and keep the same direction when it becomes a grass path. When you reach the end of a forest road the view to the right across the valley is of the woods through which you will return. Keep going the same way down to a road and turn left. The cottages here were once the homes of those who laboured in the foundries, forges, tinplate works, corn mills and chemical works which filled the valley from the 17th to the early 20th century. In about 100 yards go up a path at the back of a cottage. This was a road with houses all along on the left, only the one at the far end still has its walls standing. Continue going down and round to the widest stile west of the Severn. Follow the well-used path to the far end of the bottom field and so on to the road.

Opposite the footpath sign there used to be an enormous

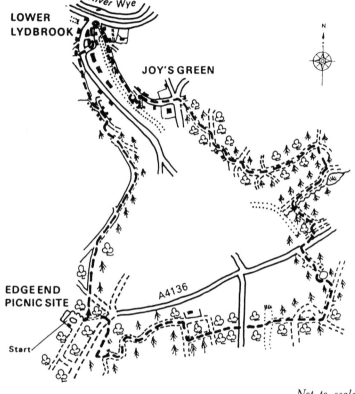

*Not to scale*

tinplate works. Cross the road, turn left and immediately turn right. This area was once crammed with buildings and would have been noisy, dusty, and full of activity. There was a large pool on the left which fed the Lydbrook Lower Forge (c1611), part of which survives in the last building on the left, opposite an inn. It was one of the first to use waterpower to drive the bellows which increased the airflow to the charcoal, thereby increasing the output many times. A 'forge' was where they smelted and hammered the pig iron from the 'furnace' to make it less brittle. It had nothing to do with horses, as depicted on the mural opposite.

Ahead is the Wye where there was a quay for shipping the finished iron, in very small boats, up to Hereford or down to the Severn. Round the corner to the right is the Courtfield Arms, a coaching inn on the turnpike road between Ross and Coleford. But on the corner there begins a long flight of steps. Go up here.

48

At the top, in 1810, there was a junction in the tramroad which came down the valley side from Mirey Stock. Here one branch went off along the hillside for a mile to Bishopswood whilst the other went down a steep incline. At this point the horses turned round and went back. The house at that time was an inn. Walk on along the lower road for 50 yards and stop before reaching the house on the right. Looking down you can see the course of the Severn and Wye Railway. To the right it suddenly comes to an end, high above valley. Here was an impressive stone viaduct where the railway crossed the valley. In 1874 it cost £7,396 to build. Beyond the house, when the track goes down, keep ahead along the course of the tramway. This path eventually leaves the tramway and goes down a flight of wooden steps to continue along the old railway. Just past the drive to the house on the left turn left to another long flight of steps. A few steps up, in the now derelict cottage on the right, there lived the widow of a miner. She related to me stories of her husband who had worked in the Waterloo mine at the time it was flooded. The men were able to escape but all the ponies perished.

At the top turn right. In 50 yards, just beyond the end of the garden of the last house on the left, look in the bank under a tree where there is the remains of a kiln. Continue to the T junction and go straight over, to turn right up a track into the wood. In ¼ mile, at the forest road, turn right and go down to a road which leads round behind some cottages. This road leads to a track into the wood and in a few yards fork right. Keep straight ahead at the next cross tracks and in ½ mile when the track – which is now a forest road – turns round to the right, and a grass track comes down from the left, turn sharp right down the valley.

At the bottom turn right. On the left is the Great How Brook, now called the Greathough Brook, with its dry pond. As you go along look for gaps in the bushes on the left where the deer go down to drink. Turn left at the first turning and stop for a moment and look around. The forester has to contend with tree pests from time to time. One is the pine shoot moth. It lays its eggs in the centre bud of the Scots pine causing it to grow out sideways and then return to the correct position for the next year. This produces a bow in the trunk which is called the 'posthorn deformation'. Can you see one?

Continue up the track, passing the turning on the right where the stonework of the old railway bridge can be seen. At the next gap on the right in a few yards, where the track continues up to the left, turn right. Follow the narrow path up to cross a forest track and, bearing slightly right, arrive at the main road (A4136).

Here turn right for 20 yards and cross – with great care. This car park is for the fishermen. If you go straight ahead to the far end and bear right you will come to the fishermen's lake. It is a serene and restful place. Walk round to the right to a small wooden bridge over a dry stream. Here turn right away from the lake and in 50 yards climb up to a forest road and turn right. Keep straight ahead up to a T junction where the electricity cables overhead turn right. Follow the cables downhill until the well-used path bears left down and across the old Severn and Wye Railway cutting.

Maintain the same direction on the other side to a road – which you will come upon suddenly. Cross this road and keep the same direction to cross straight over a forest road. Continue for ¼ mile and at the T junction with a wide grass road, turn right. In 200 yards turn left on a wide forest road.

In ¾ mile, halfway round the second sharp bend, go straight ahead. You may have to go over the stile on the right and turn left. Climb up the hill to a cross track and turn right. This will take you to a stile and a main road (A4136). Bear left across this road with great care and go up through the trees to the grass track leading to the car park where the walk started.

*Turkey Oak*

# POPE'S HILL

WALK 16

★

5 miles (8 km)

OS Landranger 162, and Outdoor Leisure 14,
Wye Valley and Forest of Dean

This is a walk in the less frequented part of the Forest of Dean, where there are some small wooded hills. Pope's Hill is 1½ miles east of Cinderford. It is signposted ½ mile from the village of Littledean on the road to Gloucester.

From the highest point of the common at Pope's Hill there is a magnificent view of the upper tidal reaches of the river Severn. It is in this part of the river that the Severn Bore starts to build up. The Heart of England Tourist Board produces an excellent information sheet with calendar, so that you can tell when and where to view this unusual sight. It is well worth seeing. Pope's Hill was an important place in the early industrial history of Dean. Before the development of waterpower to work the bellows in the 16th century, iron furnaces were built on the tops of the hills so as to make use of all the wind there was. It is difficult to imagine the smoke and fumes of a windy day where there is now only the pure air of the Severn Estuary.

Cars can be parked just clear of the wood near the T junction at the western end of the scattered village – the end nearest the wooded hill. The walk starts from here (GR: SO 682 146).

Standing at the T junction facing the wooded hill, go to the left of the garden of the house on the hillside. In a few yards, at the track, turn left. This track eventually becomes a forest road and gradually rises to go round the end of the hill. At the big bend there are a number of exposures of rock in the bank on the right. The rock can be seen to dip down to the left, as all the rocks do on this side of the Dean. On the other side of the forest the angle is reversed and is not so steep. This hill is called Chestnuts Hill from the large number of chestnut trees mixed with the oak. Were these the descendants of the trees planted for coppicing, 300 years ago, to fuel the furnaces on Pope's Hill? As you go over the hill, look about you. It is just possible to see the level platforms made by the charcoal burners as a base for their 'pits'. They have not

51

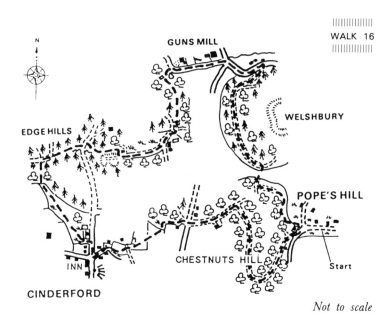

*Not to scale*

been used for many years, so in summer they may be difficult to see. They are dotted about all over the hillside. In a survey of the Dean Forest in the 13th century there were recorded over 2,000 such platforms. Today the wood is being managed to produce mature straight hardwood trees which fetch a high price. Walk on past the barrier down to the T junction and turn left. Continue on this track to the main road.

Cross the road and go up the drive towards the house opposite. A few yards before the garden gate bear right and follow a narrow path next to the hedge on the left with a field beyond. This path turns left round the top of the field and then goes to a stile. Two of the three large stone steps leading up to the stile are made of conglomerate, a natural stone formed some 100 million years ago. In the field beyond follow the path on up the hill to another stile. In the next field keep the same direction to a small notch on the skyline in the line of an old hedge. Looking back down the field it is possible to see traces of the old track which came up here and wore away the edge. Down below to the right is the 'House of Correction', built in 1790, mainly for poachers and vagrants from the forest. Beyond is Dean Hill which gives its name to the forest. Turning round again you can see the track crossing to the far corner of the field. This track was made by people going about their daily work. Similar ones are being made along the Pennines and on other long distance walks by people going about for pleasure.

As you near the far side of the field notice the flat area with the track going round it to the left. There must have been a house here connected to the road by the hedged track just beyond the stile. Go over the stile and the one opposite and keep the same direction to another stile in a wall, 5 yards to the left of the gate. What a nice idea to put a seat on the small common land. Keep the same direction up the road to the Royal Foresters Inn at the top.

A few yards along the road to the left is one of the best views of the Severn Valley. Looking up the river to the left is towards the Stroud Valley and Haresfield Beacon. Away to the right on the far side of the wide stretch of water is Slimbridge. Walk along the lane opposite the end wall of the inn towards the forest. In a little over 100 yards go up a track on the left and when it bears round to the right go over a stile to enter the corner of a rough enclosure. Follow the path up to the trees forking left as necessary. This is the land of mountain bikes, so paths appear where no path was before. So long as you are walking on the left of the open wood going downhill gently, with a view over the school playing fields on the left, you are in the right direction. Continue down to a stile on the left leading to a path through the wood. In ¼ mile this path goes to a forest road. Here turn right and at the left hand bend leave the road and go straight ahead along a well used path. This is one of the few public rights of way in the forest. At the gravel road bear left across the road and continue through the wood. This path is very steep farther down the hillside so it may be possible to go down in the valley by bearing right across the gravel road. As you descend there are old limestone quarrries on either side and a good track leading down. You eventually come to an open space with large mounds all around. On the left are the remains of two old limekilns where the limestone was burnt. Continue down the track on the right.

At the Severn Trent Water building turn left and go up a forest road. At the side of the barrier fork right onto a path which, in a few yards, crosses an old forest road now becoming overgrown. This takes you down the valley with the stream below on the right. Having walked between two very old beech trees, sadly nearing their end, the path comes to a spring with a stone surround. Was this a sediment tank or was it where the people from just down the valley came for their drinking water? Walk on out to the road and turn right. As you go down the lane there are signs of past activity on the left. First, two buildings, one with weavers' windows and the other the old mill now converted to a house. In 100 yards all that remains of another mill is a wall, now covered with ivy. At the end of the lane is Guns Mill.

When it was first built is not known but in 1683 it was being rebuilt and the present ivy-covered structure is a furnace of that date. It is subject to a building preservation order and has been surveyed by the Gloucestershire Industrial Archaeology Society, but is in danger of collapse unless money is found to make it safe. It is known to have produced almost 780 tonnes of iron in 1705, when there were also two grist mills and a fulling mill using the water from the mill pond, which alas is now dry. By 1743 it was a paper mill.

Go out to the road and take the lane ahead, signposted Flaxley. In about ¼ mile, almost opposite a green tin shed, turn right on to a track which goes up the hillside and overlooks Guns Mill. At the first left hand bend the track becomes a wide forestry road. High on the hill to the left, hidden in the trees, are the well-defined fortifications of a pre-Roman camp called Welshbury. Continue for ½ mile to where the forest road turns round the end of the wood and there is a stile on the right. Go over here and across to the opposite wood. Walk up the forest road and in 50 yards turn left along a grass track which goes round the hill. If you keep to the higher track you avoid the mud. This track eventually goes down to the opposite side of the garden you set off past at the beginning of the walk.

*White Spruce*

# SYMONDS YAT EAST

## WALK 17   4\5 .

★

8½ miles (14 km)

OS Landranger 162, and Outdoor Leisure 14,
Wye Valley and Forest of Dean

Symonds Yat is a famous beauty spot 5 miles south of Ross on Wye and 3 miles north of Coleford. The walk starts from Symonds Yat East (not to be confused with Symonds Yat West, which is on the opposite side of the river). To reach Symonds Yat East from the A40, Ross (M50) to Monmouth road, take the B4229 road to Goodrich and in ¾ mile turn right to cross a narrow metal bridge. From Coleford follow the B4432 road. Symonds Yat is well signposted from all directions.

Yat is an old local term for a gateway and Symonds comes from a High Sheriff of Herefordshire who owned much land hereabouts in the 17th century.

This walk starts at Biblins car park 1 mile south of Yat Rock off the B4432 (GR: SO 566 137). The entrance, which is down a gravel forest road, is opposite the small settlement of Hillersland.

Go out of Biblins car park on a path at the opposite end to the entrance. This takes you along the hillside to join a waymarked path, which is now a public footpath. At the first forest road turn right and in a few yards turn left. At the next forest road turn right. Cross straight over the exit road from the Symonds Yat car park and when the track forks keep to the left. On reaching the 'Pay and Display' notice, turn left down the road into the car park. On nearing the toilet block turn right.

As you go along you can see, on either side, the remains of the earthworks of the Iron Age camp which once stood on this prominent point. Walk through to the 'Disabled Car Park'. If you have not been to the view point at Yat Rock walk on past the log cabin and go over the footbridge. The walk continues by walking along the main road, away from the footbridge, to the small Symonds Yat East car park. Go straight through the park to an opening on the opposite side. This is the beginning of the 'Coldwell Walks'. Follow this good track for ¼ mile to a gate. From here the route is along a well walked path for nearly ½ mile,

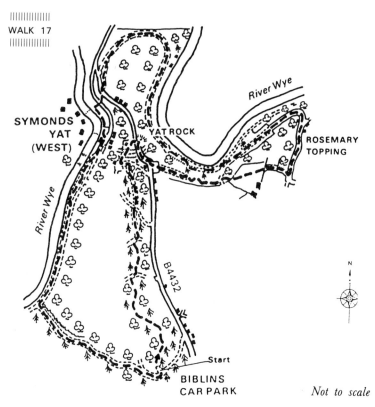

SYMONDS
YAT
(WEST)

River Wye

River Wye

YAT ROCK

ROSEMARY
TOPPING

B4432

N

Start

BIBLINS
CAR PARK

*Not to scale*

keeping near the fence on the right when possible. Pass a gate on the right and go up to a stile into a field. From here bear slightly right over the rise and go to a stile in a fence. The church on the hill opposite is at English Bicknor. Go ahead to the next stile and down the steps through the wood. At the lane turn left.

As you go down the lane you pass the drive to the house called Rosemary Topping on the left. This is also the name given to the small round hill which forms the end of the ridge. At the bottom of the hill the road turns into a track as it passes the last cottage, eventually coming to a gate and stile. Keep to the track as it goes along the bottom of a field with a wood on the right. When the wood ends there is a fine view of the Wye down below on the right. In the wood on the other side of the river is the drowned boy's memorial stone seen on Walk 21. Follow the track across the field down to a wood. When the track sweeps round to the right to a derelict barn, keep straight ahead through the wood, next to a fence on the right. At the end of the fence the track turns right onto an old railway embankment. Here turn left.

As you walk along the old railway track you come to a stile.

56

According to the map you are 100 yards from the small car park at the start of the walk – but it is also 300 ft above you.

Continue past the bricked-up entrance to the railway tunnel and soon start climbing up a forest road. In about ¼ mile there are some rough stone steps on the left. These would take you to the road just below the Yat Rock. The continuation of this path on the right of the forest road takes you down steps to a riverside walk. If this is followed it involves a very steep ascent of some 200 ft at the end of a wood, to bring you back to the forest road. Continue ahead going up and round Huntsham Hill. In about ¾ mile, on the inside of a large bend, there is an excellent example on the left of Nature's cement, the conglomerate rock. This has lasted some 100,000,000 times longer than man's equivalent. In a further ¼ mile, look on the left for a waymark sign. Follow this along the old road through the woods.

Cross the narrow road and walk uphill for 50 yards to a small passing place for cars on the right. In the middle of this passing place bear right at the footpath sign to go down to the lane at Symonds Yat East. On the lane, turn left for 20 yards and then follow a grass track across the field on the right.

At the riverside you may find a ferry working which would take you over to the Old Fleece Inn. If you do not wish to go over the river, turn left along the riverside path to the Saracen's Head, where a lower ferry operates. Continue along the side of the river past the hotels which cater for fishermen during the salmon season. Beyond the last hotel walk along the riverside path, which rises up to the old railway track, which in turn rises up to a forest road.

The river at this point has many small rapids, which in this case is the result of the island (a fallen block of lower dolomite which has encouraged silting) speeding up the river flow. It provides an excellent place for innumerable canoeists to learn how to handle their craft.

Continue until you come to a wide stone track going up a valley. At the bottom there is a sign post, to Christchurch. Turn left up this track with a deeply cut stream-bed on the left. On the left, as you ascend, there are white marker posts – if you see them you are in the right valley. About halfway up there is a path going off up to the right to Bracelands. The white markers go up here, but you keep to the main track. Eventually you will come up to the side of the car park.

# DRYBROOK

WALK 18

★

5 miles (8 km)

OS Landranger 162, and Outdoor Leisure 14,
Wye Valley and Forest of Dean

It is to this area that many university and school parties come to
study geology. The first part of the walk does a very rapid survey
of the main features which can be seen. The outward journey is
along the north eastern rim of the basin of carboniferous
limestones. It is possible to see rocks which were laid down over
a period of some six million years because they have been heaved
up to an angle of 70° in later earth movements.

The start is ½ mile west of Mitcheldean. In the middle of the
village a lane goes up the hill, signposted 'Drybrook'. The start is
also ½ mile from Drybrook, on a road from the centre of the town
signposted 'Mitcheldean'. Cars can be parked on either side of the
bend at the top of the hill (GR: SO 655 180).

On the inside of the bend is the wide entrance to a forest road and
on the outside of the bend there are two tracks. The walk begins
by going along the left hand one. This track goes to a farm just
inside the wood, the other is a good gravel road. Follow the track
into the wood, past the entrance to Stenders Farm and up the path
behind the barrier. In ¼ mile a white gate comes into sight
leading into a field. You will now be able to see, by the surface
of the track, that you are walking over sandstone. This is called
Drybrook sandstone after the village of Drybrook a mile away
behind you, where there is an enormous quarry. At the top of the
hill, follow the track round to the right past some gnarled old
beech trees which have been wind-blasted. In 200 yards look over
to the right through a gap in the trees to the quarry which
stretches all along the hillside. When you reach the lane follow it
downhill. If you are interested in the geology of the area some of
it can be seen down the road to the left. If you must get on, go
straight across the main road and miss the next paragraph.

The Forest of Dean is formed on the top of a pile of saucers
which have been tilted up at this point. Go down the main road
to just round the big bend and turn round. High up on the right

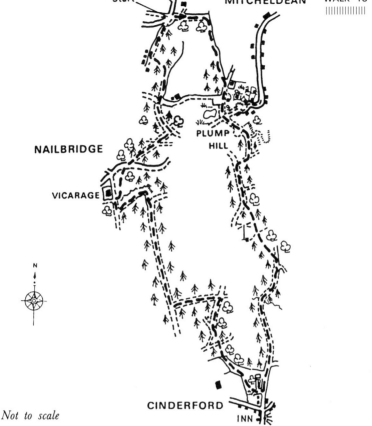

Start

NAILBRIDGE

PLUMP HILL

VICARAGE

CINDERFORD
INN

*Not to scale*

there are boulders of quartz conglomerate resting on the Tintern sandstone on which you are standing. Walk back along the pavement on the inside of the bend and 2 yards past the manhole cover (by Herbert Young of Cinderford) there is an exposure of limestone shale in the bank on the right. Notice the almost vertical bedding. At the end of the pavement cross the road and in 100 yards pass a large dolomite quarry. From just past the little chapel you can see how the rocks dip down steeply to the left. Returning to the top of the hill, turn left across the main road.

Continue ahead to the top of the hill overlooking a quarry, where you can see some of the layers of rock which are very thin at this point. You are looking at the bedding plane; this face was once horizontal. On the right of the quarry one of the 'saucers' is made of a very fine coal dust.

Follow the track into the wood and in a few yards bear right

59

onto a wide gravel forest road. Turn left and go up the hill. At the cross tracks, leave the main track and bear left to follow the overhead electricity wires up a grass track. Along this path, which goes just below a television relay station, the banks are covered with bilberries and the damp ditches are lined with an attractive lichen (cladonia). At the cross path go straight ahead. When you see old man's beard hanging in the trees you will know there is a belt of blue limestone down below. At the forest road keep ahead and at the stone road turn right. Continue until it joins a lane, where you keep straight ahead. After passing between two old gateposts, and going along the road for a short way, there is a view to the left, past a cluster of electricity poles, to the bends in the river Severn from Sharpness to above Gloucester. (The best viewing point is a little further on opposite the inn.)

Almost opposite the electricity poles in the field below the road, look on the opposite side of the road for a gravel track which curves round behind the houses you passed. Go up here and in 30 yards go over a stile on the right and follow the path, keeping to the left hand side of the ridge. This path goes down to a stile into the wood. Keep straight ahead, across a forestry track and along a pleasant grass path to merge with another forest road. In 100 yards fork right.

Continue to the cross track and turn left downhill, through a gate and at the next cross track turn right. In almost a mile, where this forest road sweeps round to the right look on the left for a path which continues down into the valley. At the end of the fence on the left, turn left and follow the path down to a wide forest road and turn right.

On reaching the bar across the track, next to an ancient beech tree, bear right up a path and follow it out to a cross path at the top of the ridge. Here turn left up to the main road. Cross with care and go through a gate into the forest opposite, to follow the yellow waymarks which bear up to the right. At the top of the dark tunnel of trees keep the same direction. At the top of the rise do not fork right but continue through the wood. In 200 yards, at the cross track, turn left.

Walk along this forest road which gradually goes down, through gates, to the corner of a field. Here turn right along the edge of the wood, to walk with the field hedge on the right. After a short distance the path gradually goes down. At the house at the bottom turn right. This rough lane used to be the main road from Monmouth to Gloucester and in the 13th century was called 'Spanneway'. It was improved by a turnpike trust in the 17th century but was later abandoned. Continue along here to the car.

# LEA BAILEY INCLOSURE

WALK 19

★

4 ½ miles (7 km)

OS Landranger 162, Pathfinder 61/71, 62/72

This walk is on a low dome of rock surrounded by hills. It is known to geologists as the Hope Mansel Dome. The centre, where the walk goes, is lower Devonian brownstones, which were folded during the inter-Caboniferous period of earth movement about 300,000,000 years ago. The surrounding hills are edged with quartz conglomerate.

The walk starts from Bailey Lane End, one of seven settlements round the dome. During the walk all the other six settlements will be visited, though two have shrunk to a few houses. Bailey Lane End can be reached either from the A40(T) Ross on Wye to Gloucester road, by turning toward Drybrook 1 mile from Weston under Penyard, or by taking the road to Ross from the centre of Drybrook, which is 2 miles north of Cinderford. The main settlement of Lane End lies below the level of the road and close up against the edge of the forest. Go down the track past the end house next to the wood and park under the trees on the right (GR: SO 643 199).

From the car go along a path leading into the wood, parallel to and about 50 yards away from the road. It starts in line with the end house and the little blue tombstones to a group of four gnomes. On reaching a gravelled area bear left to the lane, 50 yards from the T junction then turn left. In 20 yards turn right past a barrier and go ahead. In a few yards go up to the left to the beginning of an old quarry. In the right hand side of the quarry face there is a wide arch and coming out from under the iron door is a short length of track. This was Bailey Level, where iron ore was mined until 1925.

From time to time gold has been found in Dean. The conglomerates, which are of sedimentary origin, are largely made up of quartz-pebbles embedded in a red sandy matrix composed of quartz grains of various sizes. (They can be clearly seen on the side of the road to Drybrook.) The formation resembles the 'Banket' or gold-bearing conglomerates of the Transvaal and West

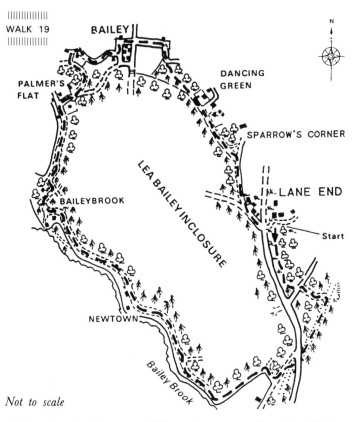

*Not to scale*

Africa, but in the case of Dean the proportion of gold is much smaller. Since 1370 various attempts have been recorded of people mining for gold, but the effort has never been economic. In 1906 gold was reported to have been discovered near Mitcheldean and an adit (a level entrance to a mine) was driven into the hillside. Both gold and silver were found but at about six grains to the ton of ore. In other words it needed 80 tons of ore to produce one ounce of gold. The exact location of this prospecting has been lost but it was not far from here.

Across the front of the quarry ran the 'Mitcheldean Road and Forest of Dean Railway' (later the GWR). Facing the quarry turn right and walk along the old railway. Go under the roadbridge and in 100 yards bear right onto a good track. In 200 yards bear right and go to the edge of the wood where there is a hedge and a field beyond. At the bottom of the slope turn left to go along a path just inside the wood. Continue along the path round the end of the wood. As you go along you will notice that the path has a good firm base. This is because it used to be a well used road.

It is marked on old maps as Elm Lane.

On reaching the cottage, you are in the centre of Newtown. The rest of the 'town' was up to the right – now covered by bracken. It had a spring called Lawer's Bath – however did it get its name? Deep inside the hill the rock is saturated with water and this comes out at various points round the dome. At each place a settlement took place. This is a reminder that until very recent times man was only able to live where there was a natural supply of water. Walk on to Baileybrook, named after the brook you have been following. Follow the track round the bends and up to a junction. Here turn left. The track eventually becomes a good road and goes down and round to the right. This is Palmer's Flat. In 200 yards, at the clearing with a house below on the left, bear left along a forest road. In ¼ mile, when a small field can be seen up on the right, look for a narrow path up to the right. This goes to the back of a cottage with a track to the right. Follow this track up to the T junction at Bailey.

Turn left along the road which turns right in 100 yards. Go straight over the crossroads. From this lane there are fine views over the countryside to the Malvern Hills and May Hill. Go round the first bend to the right and at the second to the left go straight ahead into the wood. In a few yards bear left onto a narrow path. Go down past the back of a cottage, one of the few left of Dancing Green. Walk across an open space and up a hollow way. This was once part of the road which went round the dome. At the top of the rise the track joins a well used gravel road. To the left this goes to where the settlement of Sparrow's Corner once stood, now just one large house. Continue to the right to go down to the main road at Lane End.

# LOWER LYDBROOK

WALK 20

★

6½ miles (10.5 km)

OS Landranger 162, and Outdoor Leisure 14,
Wye Valley and Forest of Dean

This walk can be combined with Walk 21 to make a longer riverside walk of 10 miles.

The walk starts from what used to be called Lydbrook Junction, but now that the railway has disappeared it has lost its name. About ½ mile along the road towards English Bicknor from Lower Lydbrook, at the turning to Upper Stowfield, there is a section of old road which was left when the new road was made at the time the railway bridge was dismantled. This old road makes an excellent place to park (GR: SO 591 175). A little further along the road to English Bicknor is a sharp bend and the entrance to Reed Corrugated Cases Ltd.

Cross the road and follow the footpath sign to Welsh Bicknor. You are now in Gloucestershire so on the hill behind you is English Bicknor. Across the river is part of south Herefordshire, which used to be subject to Welsh law, so the area is called Welsh Bicknor.

Go down the track at the side of the factory. Continue to the disused railway bridge and go up the bank on the left to cross to the other side of the Wye. The plant growing in the river is water crowfoot. At the end of the bridge go down to the right by the side of the river. Pass the house on the left and follow the path up to the left to the old vicarage, now a youth hostel.

Bear right and go down the path in front of the hostel. The church on the left was built in 1859 and paid for mostly by the rector. Now follow the path along the side of the river. In ¼ mile you are opposite Lower Lydbrook. Here there is a sudden drop in water level, where the river runs over a hard outcrop of rock. The river is made to run fast against the nearside bank and this is causing the inside of the curve to be worn away. Usually it is the outside bank which is eroded. There is also an island starting to grow in mid-stream. The group of buildings high up on the left as you walk along belong to the Mill Hill Fathers. It used to be the home of Cardinal Vaughan.

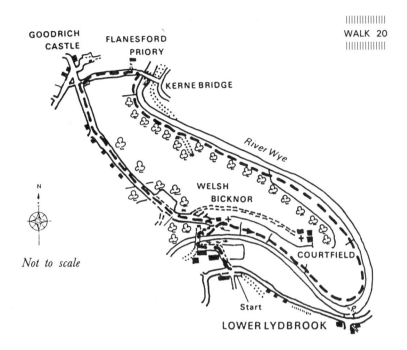

GOODRICH CASTLE  FLANESFORD PRIORY  KERNE BRIDGE  River Wye  WELSH BICKNOR  N  Not to scale  COURTFIELD  Start  LOWER LYDBROOK

As you go along the meadows you can just see, high up on the opposite hillside, the line of the old tramway from Lydbrook to Bishopswood. Just below Bishopswood, where there is now a collection of chalets, was a wharf called Cinderhill Wharf, from the mountain of cinders left by earlier workers. These were reused in the furnaces at Lydbrook, or ground up to make the well known Bristol glass, so there are none left now. Two furnaces up the hillside were operating before 1602 and at one time this was a busy part of the river.

Continue by the side of the river through a wood. When you come to a stone wall on the left, you are at the place where the Ross – Monmouth line crossed. On emerging from the wood, follow the path to Kerne Bridge. Nearby there used to be a ferry and the story is that when Henry IV was here, a messenger arrived who told him of the birth of his son, later Henry V. In great joy the King gave the messenger, whose name was Kerne, the rights of the ferry. There is no record of the comments of the original ferryman.

Go up the steps. Now take great care emerging on to the road. Turn left, keeping close against the hedge until you are on the footpath. In a few yards there is a good view of the farm across the field on the right, which used to be Flanesford Priory. It was founded by Richard Talbot – who came from a notable Midland

65

family – in 1346 when he obtained possession of Goodrich Castle through his wife. Continue up the road and climb up the path at the side of the bridge.

The entrance to Goodrich Castle is 100 yards down the road on the right. Ye Olde Hostelrie is 100 yards further. This is a romantic inn, with its Gothic windows and pinnacles, built in 1830. Was it copied from an old missal? It is interesting to discover that it was moulded in the same fashion as Goodrich Court, now mercifully demolished, which stood on the next promontory to the castle. When Wordsworth saw it he called it 'an impertinent structure'. On the A40 (T) there still stands the gatehouse, complete with machicolated towers and portcullis. The castle is in a unique position. It is built of the sandstone quarried from the dry moat. From the path to the castle you can get a good idea of the labour involved in its construction.

For your return walk you have a choice of two routes. The longer is through the old part of Goodrich and then along the riverside to the youth hostel, a distance of 5 miles. The short route is over the hill by road to the youth hostel, a distance of 1½ miles.

To follow the longer route, turn to Walk 21 and omit the first paragraph.

To follow the shorter route, walk up the lane over the road bridge. As you walk along the hillside there are magnificent views down to the river Wye. Keep to the lane over the hill and down the other side through the fields of the Courtfield estate. Keep to the right each time the road forks and go down towards the youth hostel. When you see a sign directing you down a public footpath, go down to the front of the buildings and turn right to the river and the railway bridge. Retrace you steps past the paper factory to the car.

# GOODRICH CASTLE

WALK 21

★

6½ miles (10.5 km)

OS Landranger 162, and Outdoor Leisure 14,
Wye Valley and Forest of Dean

This walk can be combined with Walk 20 to make a longer walk
of 9 miles.

Goodrich Castle stands high on a promontory overlooking the
river Wye, 3 miles south of Ross on Wye. It is well signposted as
an ancient monument on the A40 trunk road and the B4234 south
of Ross. There is an extensive car park and picnic area from
which the walk starts (GR: SO 575 193).

Leave the car park and go back down the entrance road to the
village. In winter, check to see what time the car park closes.
There will be a notice hanging at the entrance.

Cross straight over the crossroads and bear left to go down the
lane with the school on the right. Just beyond these buildings turn
right through a small gate and cross the well mown playing field.
In the next field follow the path up the bank to the left hand
corner. Now go across another rough field and into a tidy
churchyard. Go round to the south of the church and opposite the
porch there is the stump of an old cross, dated 1692. Continue
through the churchyard, across a paddock and on to a lane. In 50
yards, at the T junction by the black and white house, turn right.
On reaching the Cross Keys Inn, with its attractive little mounting
block to make it easier for riders to mount their horses, turn left
along the track at the side of the house opposite the inn. At the
end of the track go through the gate ahead into a field. Follow the
wall on the left and then curve to the left towards the left hand
end of the wood in front. Pass about 20 yards to the left of the
massive old oak standing alone in the field. At the wood turn right
following the hedge round the field. On the other side of the hedge
is a sewage works, so you may have to hurry. After turning left
and then right you will find a stile in the corner of the field. From
here you have a good view of both Symonds Yats. 'Yat' means a
gate, and Symonds was a 17th century property owner in the
district. Bear left across a field and go down to the left of a house

67

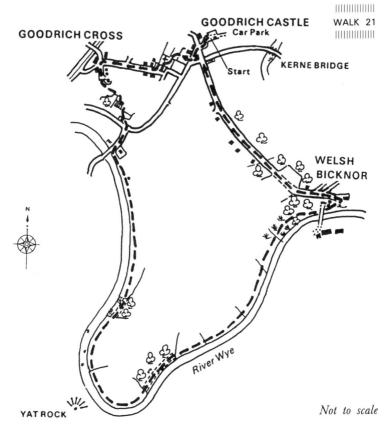

GOODRICH CASTLE

GOODRICH CROSS

Car Park

Start

KERNE BRIDGE

WELSH BICKNOR

N

River Wye

YAT ROCK

*Not to scale*

and garden to the road. Walk along the lane opposite, signposted to Symonds Yat East.

At the iron bridge go down a path at the side of the bridge and turn left. Now follow the path, which improves after a few yards, along the side of the river. On the left is Coppet Hill and here you can see the line where the conglomerate outcrops. The blocks in the river are lumps which have broken off from a continuation of the seam in the cliffs across the river. In ½ mile go through a small wood and then into meadows again. This is the place that people can see when standing at the viewpoint at Yat Rock. If you look up at the top of the rock in front you may see a row of small heads peering down at you. As you go round the bend you will see a number of the rocks standing out of the trees across the river. It is lower dolomite, a type of limestone laid down 320 million years ago – for those who would like to know, it has the chemical formula $(Ca\ Mg)\ CO_3$, which tells its own story.

Again enter a wood to find all the trees are covered with

traveller's joy, better known in autumn as old man's beard. About 100 yards inside the wood there is giant sweet chestnut tree on the left, its bark spiralling round the trunk like some gigantic gear wheel. A little further on look for a small railed-off tomb-like memorial on the left. It was erected in 1804 to John Whitehead Warre, when this five-year-old lad drowned in the Wye. '. . . This monument is here erected to warn parents and others, to be careful how they trust this deceitful stream. Particularly to exhort them to learn and observe the directions of the Humane Society for the recovery of persons apparently drowned. Alas it is with extreme sorrow, here commemorated, what anguish is felt from the want of this knowledge . . .'

Continue on through the wood and then through meadows. The wooded hill on the right is called Rosemary Topping. Look out for dragonflies in summer. In ¾ mile the path winds through scrub and then along at the bottom of a wood. Pass under the old railway bridge. In 100 yards the path starts to rise up towards the youth hostel. On reaching the hostel you have a choice of routes. To continue along the riverside path back to Goodrich is 4 miles. To go over the hill by road is 1½ miles.

If you wish to follow the Wye Valley Walk along by the river, turn to Walk 20 and omit the first two paragraphs.

The short way back is by the track up from the hostel, which improves and becomes a quiet road as it goes over the hill. Do not miss the fine views of the river Wye, far below on the right.

*Sweet Chestnut*

# WELSH NEWTON COMMON

## WALK 22

★

5½ miles (9 km)

OS Landranger 162, and Outdoor Leisure 14,
Wye Valley and Forest of Dean

Welsh Newton lies on the A466, Monmouth – Hereford road, 3 miles north of Monmouth. The A466 winds in a narrow valley as it leaves Monmouth and the church and a few houses are next to this road. The walk starts from Welsh Newton Common which is ¾ mile away on the hill, behind the church. Leave the A466 by the church and take the road up the hill which is signposted Llangarron. In ½ mile, at the top of the hill, turn right to Welsh Newton Common. Continue along the very winding lane for ½ mile and at the fork, with its red telephone box, bear right. In a further 200 yards the County Council has erected a smart bus shelter. Cars may be parked in this part of the common, making sure not to obstuct the access to any of the houses. The walk will start from the bus shelter (GR: SO 512 178).

Walk along the stone track opposite the bus shelter and pass the village shop and the water tower on the right. When the track turns right you turn left along a grass track. The view from the gateway on the right is towards Cardiff, with Monmouth hidden behind trees on the left. In a few yards go through the trees and bear left along a track. As you near the end of the track there is a group of beech trees on the left. It was from here, some years ago, before the surrounding hedges and trees had grown so high, that it was possible to see nine counties on a clear day. At the T junction turn right to go past a farm. Continue along the narrow hedged lane for ½ mile. Away to the left is St Wolstan's Farm with its enormous grain silo, sited on high ground next to the farm.

At the end of the lane bear right along a track between hedges. This used to be a continuation of the lane along the ridgeway and eventually down to Monmouth. In ¼ mile there is a wood on the right and a few yards further on a wood begins on the left. Here turn left and go down just inside the wood. The footpath should be a few yards to the left of the present track, but until it is

N

INN
LLANGROVE

LITTLE HALL

WELSH
NEWTON
COMMON — Start

ST WOLSTAN'S
FARM

LEWSTONE

*Not to scale*

cleared of the trees, bushes and brambles, keep to the track. In 200 yards the track forks. At this point look to the left for a narrow path through the bushes. Go along this path for a few feet to a gate and from here continue down the hill on the correct line of the footpath, which is a wide hedged grass track. In 200 yards go over a stile into a field and continue with the hedge on the left. Notice how this hedge was built on top of a bank, which might have started life as a stone wall. Was this once an old boundary? Pass through a gate and in a further 100 yards go over a stile on the left, so as to walk with the hedge on the right. Go past the house called Great Hillshone and follow the hedge on the right down into Lewstone.

Turn left along the lane marked as a 'no through road' and in ¼ mile pass a house on the left. The lane now becomes a hedged track and goes downhill, to become no more than a footpath at the bottom of the hill. The hedge plants on either side have now grown up into trees or have been stifled and died. Continue up the valley with the brook sometimes close by on the right and sometimes below across a field. The path eventually turns back and into a grass way used by the farmer to reach the surrounding

71

fields. On reaching a gate across the track you will see ahead no trace of the hedged road you have been following for nearly a mile. Ordnance Survey maps of the beginning of this century show two hedges going up the hillside in front. How easy it is for the countryside to change and leave no trace of its previous design. Looking round the hillside we find that many of the hedges round the fields are not more than 200 years old and for a long time before that these parts were subject to Celtic husbandry. Near Lewstone, out in the middle of a field, was once found a tessellated pavement – there may be more below the surface of these hills. We also know from aerial photography and archaeological field work that land shortage was becoming a problem as long ago at 500 BC. How many times have these hills known a change of clothing?

From the gate into the field bear left to go halfway up the side of the round-topped hill. Go over a stile in a fence and aim for a point halfway down the right hand hedge. The stile is hidden from view by the overhang of a tree. On the lane beyond turn left. In 200 yards when the lane goes round to the left keep straight ahead to a gate. From here the route goes over a stile and up this valley to the left of a dried-up watercourse as far as the corner. Cross the footbridge and stile onto the end of a track which gradually improves until it comes out onto the main road through Llangrove.

At this point, should you need a rest, you will find a pleasant circular seat under the tree on the corner. Across the road is the 1887 village water supply. Turn left along the road past the church and in 300 yards pass the Royal Arms inn. In a further 100 yards turn left along a lane, with a high garden wall on the left. Pass the imposing entrance gates and notice the name of the dwelling. In 200 yards at the fork, turn right and in a further 100 yards turn left downhill. Follow this old road for 1 mile as it winds across the valley and up to the top of the hill opposite.

The first house you reach is Little Hall, the second is Great Hall, and in 200 yards there is a fine view over the valley to the wooded hills of Great and Little Doward. Continue to the entrance gates of Newton Lodge. Do not follow the lane round to the right but cross in front of the gates and keep next to the wall on the left. This leads to a narrow walled path, actually a part of the common, which soon widens out. Pass the cottage on the right and go straight over the track, to follow a path next to a hedge on the right. This soon becomes a hedged track, though the hedges are rather unusual. Five yards before reaching the lane, turn left in front of the houses and go along a grass track which runs parallel to the narrow lane. In 100 yards you emerge onto the open common next to the bus shelter, where the walk started.

# ROSS ON WYE: PENYARD PARK

WALK 23

★

6 miles (9.5 km)

OS Landranger 162, Pathfinder 62/72

This walk starts from the town of Ross and goes over the hill which towers behind it. Ross is the last town the river Wye passes before it enters the confines of the Forest of Dean. The town stands on the road from central England to the southern parts of Wales. It has always had the benefit of passing trade, with cattle and sheep going east or people going west. It is also an important local centre for farmers, as it still has a thriving market.

The M50, a westerly spur of the M5, ends just outside the town. Travellers from the south have a choice of two routes, to go through Monmouth or Coleford.

There are many small car parks round the town and it is only a short walk from any of them to the churchyard, where the walk starts (GR: SO 598 240).

From the row of attractive houses which line the north side of the churchyard, go to the left of the church to a small metal gate in the wall near a silver birch tree.

Keep straight ahead down a road, with first a clinic and then a police station on the left, and at the bottom, on the right, is the site of the old toll-gate. Bear left across the main road and continue past Dean Hill Hospital on the left. This road has an interesting collection of domestic architecture of all sizes, from the very old to the very new. Go down the hill until you come to a factory estate on the right. Here turn right along Penyard Lane.

Walk along the lane for ¼ mile to Alton Court. That which is seen from the entrance gate is genuine 16th century, but the rear of the building, as seen from further back down the road, should not be looked at closely. Continue by going through a wicket gate at the end of the lane, signposted 'Wye Valley Walk'. Follow the well trodden path till it goes through small metal gates into the bottom of a field. Immediately turn right and go up the field keeping about 20 yards from the hedge on the right. As you start to go up you will see a sandstone fortress-like building coming into view, just to the left. As you climb higher you will become

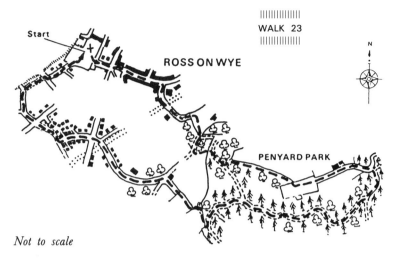

Start

ROSS ON WYE

PENYARD PARK

N

*Not to scale*

disillusioned. It is the front of a corrugated iron cover to a water tank. At the top of the field go over a stile which leads to a track ahead. Follow the track until it comes out into a field.

Here you leave the Wye Valley Walk and turn left up the side of the wood. At the top bear left across the field up to a stile. This is Penyard Wood. From the stile go up the bank to the forest road and turn right. Follow this forest road for ¼ mile. At the top of the rise look on the left for a small track which goes up to a gate with a field beyond. Go up here and just before reaching the gate turn right along the edge of the wood with the fence on the left. Note: the field on the other side of the fence is a danger area connected with the rifle range in the valley below the castellated water tank!

Look on the oaks on the right for galls. In spring these are tiny round pinkish-brown balls which the gall wasp, a small solitary waisted wasp, induces the oak to grow when it lays its egg at the base of a leaf. Inside the gall is a grub and later the grub makes its way to the surface and turns into an insect, leaving a neat round hole the size of a pin head to show where it emerged. By winter the gall has turned dark brown and become very hard.

At the bottom of the wood go over the stile on the right of the gate and into a field. On the other side of the field, where there are some large trees in the wood, is the site of Penyard Castle. Built in the 14th century, it belonged to the Talbot family but was in ruins by the 17th century.

Turn left along the field to a gate and on to the end of a lane. Walk along the lane past the farm on the left. In the wall of the barn, near the far end, you can see some pieces of carved stone. These must surely have come from the ruined castle. This is what happened to many of our ancient monuments, for they have so much of their building stone missing. The whole farm was probably built of free second-hand stone. Continue for a further ¼ mile and at the sharp left hand bend, where the lane goes steeply downhill, turn right and follow the path down through the trees. In ¾ mile fork right on to a forest road which goes uphill.

As the track goes round a sharp left hand bend the tall oaks at the top of the wooded slope, which can just be seen through the trees, are those at Penyard Castle. In ½ mile, at a meeting of tracks – some old, some new – go straight ahead. As you go down you pass a turning to the left and in a few yards, when you are at the bottom of the slope, look on the right for a path through the bushes. You will be able to see the corner of a field and a stile. The wood here used to extend a few yards further than it does today. Go over the stile and turn right. Follow the fence up to where there is a metal gate in the corner of the field 20 yards over to the left. Walk over the undulations to a stile next to the gate. Keep ahead up the bank and follow the hedge to a stile in the corner. Beyond this turn right along what used to be a good track. In summer you can tell it was once a stone track because the grass does not grow so well where there is only a shallow layer of soil and in dry weather the grass along this strip tends to turn yellow. From an aircraft it betrays its past history. Archaeologists call it a 'parch mark'. Walk on up a sunken track to a road junction and go straight over on the road down the hill. Walk on down the road to the main road (B4234) and cross to go down Roman Way. Continue almost as far as the right hand bend and turn right between house number 55 and 57. This is a well surfaced path which takes you to a road. Cross straight over along Cleeve Way, which turns into a track and then forks. Bear right.

When the track starts to go downhill, turn right up a flight of steps. Follow the path along the edge of two fields to another track. Turn right and in 20 yards, at the end of a wooden fence, turn left up some more steps. Notice the old gas lamp post – alas, not working – and the two hinged arms on which the lamp man put his ladder. Continue along this path until it reaches the churchyard from which you started.

# ROSS ON WYE: BRAMPTON ABBOTTS

## WALK 24

★

5½ miles (9 km)

OS Landranger 162, Pathfinder SO 52/53, 62/63

This walk starts from the town of Ross and visits the village of Brampton Abbots, returning by the side of the river. There are ample official parking places all round the town, which is not so large that a stranger will get lost, yet large enough to provide the amenities a modern community needs. This prosperous little town owes much of its character to its best known inhabitant who was born in 1637. He was John Kyrle, known locally as the 'Man of the Ross'. Pope, in his *Moral Essays*, extols Kyrle's virtues with great feeling and without his usual satire, so he must have merited more than most men of his time (Epistle III, lines 250-300). The church of St Mary stands high, overlooking the Wye Valley. Go into the churchyard to start the walk (GR: SO 598 240).

From the row of attractive houses which line the town side of the churchyard, go down the wide steps at the western corner and turn right. At the main road through the town turn left. In 50 yards turn right to go down Edde Cross Street. There are a number of interesting buildings and features on this road. At the bottom of the hill, at the T junction, cross straight over, to go up a 'no through road' and under a bridge.

In a few yards fork right up a well used footpath which climbs up the hill to come out onto a road. Turn left past modern Ross. At the top of the hill the road crosses over the dual carriageway of the link road connecting the M50 and A40. From here you can see excellent exposures of old red sandstone on either side of the cutting. In a further 300 yards the road turns sharply to the right, but you keep straight ahead down a rough lane. This curves across the valley to the hamlet of Netherton.

Straight ahead is the corner of a field which has a farm gate with a kissing gate on its right. Go through here, up the bank and across the field, past a second kissing gate in the hedge on the right. This type of gate was very popular in Georgian and Victorian England, as it formed a matching part of the iron railings round an estate. It enables people to get through but not

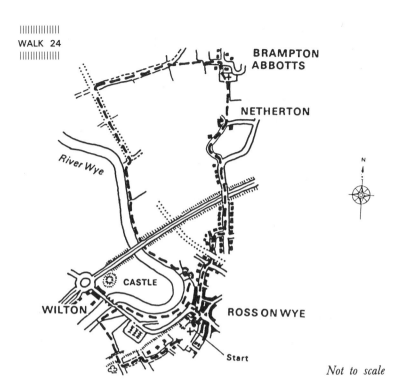

BRAMPTON
ABBOTTS

NETHERTON

River Wye

N

CASTLE

WILTON

ROSS ON WYE

Start

*Not to scale*

animals. The gates were usually only 3 ft high, thus facilitating the more important function from which they derive their name. There are a number of these gates around Ross and most of them are in good order, having been renewed within recent years. Perhaps the demand for this design is greater here than in most parishes. Continue along the path, next to the fence on the right, into the churchyard at Brampton Abbotts. Pass to the left of the church and then bear left into the corner of the churchyard. From here a narrow path goes past the School House to a small gate. Go through this gate and immediately turn left to follow the footpath sign.

Keep straight ahead and go over the fence to follow the hedge on the right. When the hedge ends keep the same direction down to the corner of the field, where there is a stile onto a track. Keep the same direction along this track for ½ mile. At the old railway track the right of way goes ahead and then to the left through two meadows. But this is not now used as the Wye Valley Walk uses the old railway track, so turn left along this track. In ½ mile, when the track ends, follow the waymarks down to the right and along the riverside.

In another ½ mile you go under the dual carriageway road that you went over on the way out. Walk on along the next meadow as far as the electricity pole and then bear left. This path goes round behind the boathouse, crossing two bridges, each with their gates. Is it a sign of the times that the leaders of the parish have authorised spikes to be placed on top of kissing gates? Continue through the park next to the river, passing the garden of the Hope and Anchor Inn on the left.

When you come to a waymarked post which shows that the Wye Valley Walk goes off to the left, keep ahead. In ¼ mile you can just see the remains of Wilton Castle, hidden in the trees, on the opposite side of the river. This is a genuine medieval castle, whereas that which graces the sandstone heights overlooking the river is an elaborate 1840 'medievalisation'. Pass under the end arch of Wilton bridge. This was built in 1597 and is a fine example of 16th century workmanship, with its massive cutwaters and ribbed arches. It has been skilfully widened to take motor traffic. In the centre of the parapet, there is an 18th century sundial with the inscription:

> 'Esteem thy precious time
> Which pass so swift away
> Prepare thee for eternity
> And do not make delay.'

Continue along the riverside for 200 yards and then turn left over a stile. In the meadow beyond keep ahead, with the hedge on the left. At the far end of the meadow there is a stile which leads to a path which turns into a track as it goes up in a cutting through the sandstone cliff. As you go up you come to two flights of steps following the path to the next track in a cutting. Here turn right for 20 yards and then turn left again to follow the path which eventually arrives in the corner of the churchyard.

As you go through the churchyard look over to the left where there is a Georgian arch. This was the south gate of The Prospect, a public garden which once occupied all the ground to the south, west and north of the church and is still a monument to Kyrle's generosity, though only a fraction of the original imaginative layout remains. It was because of this and his many charitable actions that he became known as the 'Man of Ross'.

# SELLACK

## WALK 25

★

7 miles (11 km)

OS Landranger 162, 165,
Pathfinder SO 42/52, 62/72, 43/53, 63/73

Sellack is a tiny settlement 3 miles north-west of Ross on Wye. It is best reached from the Ross – Hereford road. From the roundabout at Wilton where the A449 (continution from the M50) meets the A40 to Monmouth, go along the A49 Hereford road. Take the second turning on the right in ¼ mile, signposted to Hoarwithy. The turning to Sellack and Baysham is in 2 miles, which is halfway between Hoarwithy and Ross. In a further ¾ mile turn left past Sellack school on a narrow lane down to the church and two houses. The walk is along fields bordering the river Wye as it makes one of its great meanders.

The church of Sellack is dedicated to St Tysilo, a little known saint in England – but much of this side of the Wye is Welsh. About ¼ mile further west from the church is Caradoc Court which is part stone and part timber, dating back to the 16th century.

The car can be parked on the grass verge near the churchyard wall (GR: SO 565 277). Keep well clear of the lane and gateways. The lane is used by farm vehicles which seem to get bigger and bigger each year.

Walk on round the churchyard wall. If the sun is shining and you want to know the time, the Georgian sundial on the tower can be read from the road but don't forget to allow for summer time if necessary. Pass the ruins on the left and at the end of the churchyard wall go over a stile next to the corner of the churchyard. From here you can see the top of a magnificent footbridge across the fields. When you cross this bridge go gently, there is an interesting movement under your feet if you go quickly! This magnificent footbridge is similar to one at Foy you cross on the way back. Could it have replaced a ferry? The houses you pass on the road ahead are in the parish of Kings Caple and form a small settlement marked on the map as Sellack Boat. Turn right at the road and in ½ mile, at the T junction, turn right past

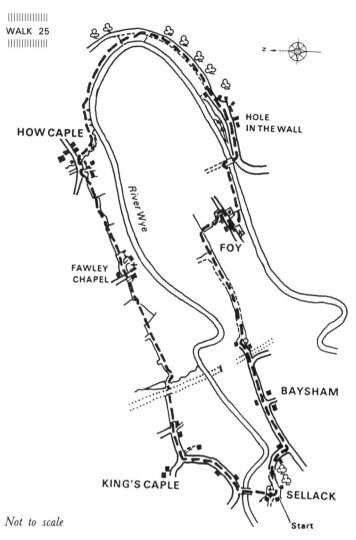

HOLE IN THE WALL

HOW CAPLE

River Wye

FOY

FAWLEY CHAPEL

BAYSHAM

*Not to scale*

KING'S CAPLE

SELLACK

Start

the entrance to Poulstone Court. When the road makes a sharp bend to the left, leave it and go straight ahead, following the sign 'Public Bridleway'. Pass the cottage and go through a gate. Walk along the next field near the hedge on the left and go under the old railway bridge.

Cross the stream and bear right. As you go up the bank, notice the hollow way in the bushes on the left, this leads to a deserted farm settlement 100 yards ahead. There are signs in the grass around here of flat areas – they may have been rick platforms or timber framed buildings which just sit on the ground, leaving no trace when they come to the end of their days. On the left of the hollow was the farmyard; the brick wall on the right went round three sides and supported the buildings. Farmyards in poorer settlements got deeper and deeper because every year a thick layer of manure was dug out and spread on the fields.

Continue in the same direction past the stumps of elms which have been attacked by Dutch elm disease. As you go along, look over to the ridge on the right on the other side of the river – you will walk along the top of this on the way back. In the far corner of the field, by the well shaped oak tree, go through a gate. From here the bridleway goes across the field to the far side through a gate and along just below the hedge on the left, to the lane at Fawley. Fawley church, with its Norman chancel arch, is down the lane and then left. The court dates back to the 16th century and the house Much Fawley has 14th century cruck trusses. This is almost all there is at Fawley.

Cross the lane and with the wall on the right pass the entrance to Seabournes. Go forward to a gate into the old farmyard. Walk on up into the field on the right and continue with the hedge on the left. Go through the gates with care as modernity is everywhere – after the string vest, the string hinge! About ½ mile past the farmyard there is an oak tree standing out in the field 5 yards from the hedge. Just past this go over a broken-down fence on the left of a gate. Go through into the field on the left and follow the hedge on the right down the hill. When the hedge ends there is a gate in front. Go through this and keep next to the fence on the left to a gate near a cottage. Here the bridlepath bears left across the field down to a road, not down the track ahead.

At the road turn right and in 100 yards turn right through a gate into a field. Walk across this field keeping about 20 yards from the hedge on the right. You are now on the Wye Valley Walk, which is well waymarked and well walked. Now follow the path along the side of the river or walk on the unfenced road a little higher up. In ½ mile you come to Hole-in-the-wall, as you will see on the post box at the far end of the cottages. It is an old box as it has VR on it, even though it looks as good as new. Pass the River Wye Canoe Centre, opposite which are some islands that are fast turning into riverside meadows. Only at flood time are they again islands and in another 100 years the land will be almost level.

Walk on along to the footbridge and cross. At the other side turn left and walk along the riverside path to the beginning of the third field. On the right the church stands high with the old vicarage next to it. From this point they look as if they are joined together but they are actually quite far apart. The right of way here turns right and goes out to the road. A parish path to the church goes to a gate in the churchyard wall. Just inside the churchyard there is a well placed seat which provides a very pleasant prospect of lush watermeadows and wooded hills. The south door of the church is 14th century and has hinges ornamented in the form of sickles. It is a well maintained centre of worship serving a mere handful of families, but is a good example of our English heritage and worthy of support. Go out through the car park to the road and turn right. Walk on along the road. This is Foy.

In 200 yards, at the far end of the farm buildings, turn left into the farmyard and go across to the left hand gate. Go through and walk next to the hedge on the right for 100 yards to a gate in front. After negotiating this go up the field with the hedge on the left. At the top of the field there is a small covered reservoir. You have to go over or round this to a gap in the end hedge. In the next field turn left and keep this direction along the top of the ridge for 1 mile. Fortunately in the second field there is a track to follow. There is a good view of Fawley to the right, where you were on the way out. Ross is to the left and the mountains of Wales in front. At the farm buildings go round to the right of the pond and continue along a stony roadway. The cottages on the left have a row of martins' nests under the eaves; these birds need to be house trained. Continue along a metalled road over the old railway bridge where the cutting has lately been filled in making it difficult to imagine what it was like in the 1950s when it was the main line from Hereford to Ross.

At the lane keep straight ahead. In ¼ mile you go through Baysham! A little further on you come to the turning for Sellack. Turn right, pass the school and go down the hill to the church.

# HOARWITHY

## WALK 26

★

4½ miles (7 km)

OS Landranger 149, Pathfinder SO 43/53

The first part of this walk is along the side of the river and the return is through quiet trackways.

The village of Hoarwithy has many of its houses built on the steep hillside overlooking the river. The church, which dominates the village, was completed in 1890 and the 'scheme for decoration' was by George Fox who also worked at Longleat. The metal bridge over the Wye is quite modern, there being no bridge in 1803. At this time there were four ferries between Hereford and Ross but it is a shallow river with many fording places.

The village of Hoarwithy is 6 miles south of Hereford at an ancient crossing of the Wye. It is signposted on the A49(T) Hereford – Ross road and also on the B4224 Hereford – Mitcheldean road.

Cars can be parked at the river side of the road, ½ mile from the centre of the village, on the road to Carey and Bolstone, opposite a wood on the hillside (GR: SO 554 304).

The walk starts from the corner of a large uneven field where there is a footpath sign, and goes to the riverbank. You will see a great ditch sweeping around to the left. This was at one time a part of the river and the footpath goes over what was once a group of islands. It was only in the middle of the last century that it began to dry out and the parish boundary still follows the ditch. Continue for 1 mile to the pillars of the old bridge which took the Hereford to Ross railway over the river. The railway was almost straight but, owing to the meanders of the river, it crossed the river three times in 2½ miles. At the stile just beyond the embankment, look across at the opposite hedge. Halfway up to the left, it will be seen to turn sharp right for 50 yards, before continuing on up the slope. A hedged track used to end at this point. The footpath goes across the field and then along the track. If there is a standing crop you may find it preferable to go into the next field to reach the track but the right of way is across the first field. Follow the track up the hill to the lane and then turn left.

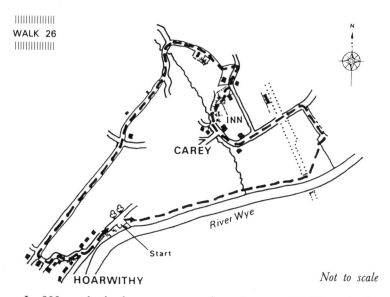

N

CAREY

INN

River Wye

Start

HOARWITHY

*Not to scale*

   In 200 yards the lane goes over the railway track. There is the office block converted to cottages on one side and on the other side the goods yard, where the local farm produce was loaded for Hereford. Continue down the lane past Rock Farm into Carey. Do not turn left at the Cottage of Content but keep straight ahead, following the stream to the first sharp left hand bend. Here turn right and cross the footbridge. Go up a flight of steps and then turn left to a gate. The path now winds along the bottom of a steep bank for 50 yards. Turn right up the bank when you come to a well used path up to the field above and then bear left up to the top corner, where the path winds between brambles to a stile If you look down below on the left there is an old overgrown road coming up from Carey. It went a few yards ahead and then turned right just in front of the bank to go through a gate. Walk up the field and go through this gate.

   Continue ahead up the road, past Carey Court on the right. At the end of the first field on the left, at the footpath sign, go into the field and follow the hedge on the right to a gate. In the next field there are fine views over the valley. Bear right along the top of this field to the corner. Enter a hedged track and then go downhill past the old buildings of Mountboon Farm. The old farmhouse has gone but the barns have been turned into a modern house, which is now called Barn House. Go down the track to the lane and turn left. In the bottom of the valley the lane goes over a stream. Until quite recently this was a ford. Many of the Herefordshire lanes had fords, in fact quite a lot still do, but motor cars and lorries do not like going through water – the horse and cart thought nothing of going through 2 ft of swirling stream. Continue up the hill and take the right fork. This used to be an important road but, as you will see, it soon becomes a hedged track, only fit for tractors. Cross the lane and keep with the track over the hill. As you go down the hill you can see the river below Hoarwithy. The church spire on the hill to the left is at Kings Caple. On reaching the lane turn left. Go downhill to the road, turn left and, keeping to the right hand side of the road, return to the car.

*Silver Birch*

# BRINKLEY HILL

WALK 27

★

2½ miles (4 km)

OS Landranger 149, Pathfinder 43/53, 63/73

Brockhampton is a small hamlet 6 miles south east of Hereford. It lies on the east side of the river Wye, well away from any main roads. To reach it from the north and west, leave the B4224 road through Fownhope and turn along a lane past the church, signposted to Capler. Turn right at the first crossroads and continue for ¾ mile. From the south and east leave the A40 at the roundabout 2 miles from the end of the M50 and go on the A49 towards Hereford. In ½ mile at the second turning on the right, go towards Hoarwithy and then bear right to cross the metal bridge over the Wye. In ½ mile turn left, signposted Brockhampton, and continue for 2 miles.

This pleasant and easy walk starts from the Brinkley Hill car park and picnic site provided by the Wye Valley Countryside Service, off the road between Brockhampton and Hoarwithy (GR: 584 313). The picnic site is ¾ mile from the new church (by Lethaby 1902), with its thatched lychgate. (Not the original church which is in ruins and can be found south of Brockhampton Court.)

Walk along the road towards Brockhampton as directed by the sign 'Wye Valley Walk 500m'. (The 'm' stands for metres, not miles!) When you reach the wall of the school playground, fork left to go behind the school. This rough lane soon turns into a grass track between high hedges. After ¼ mile, pass a cottage on the right and notice the fine views down to the left. Continue to the lane and turn left. In a few yards, opposite Capler Lodge, there is a small viewpoint constructed by the Brockhampton Court Estate, but now managed by the Countryside Service. From the right hand side of this small area you can see a track going up from the river through the wood. This is the route you will take at the end of the walk. Go on past the lodge and the wooden farm-type gates beyond. There is a path through here up to Capler Camp, one of the many prehistoric earthworks in the area. Unfortunately it is not possible to see very much of the camp as the right of way goes along a part of one side only.

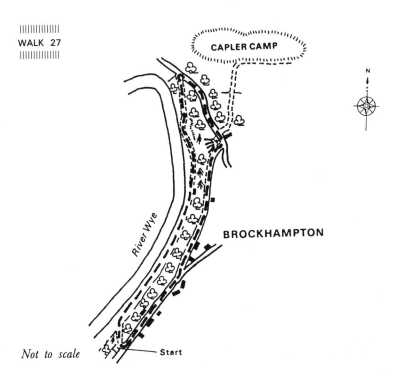

N

CAPLER CAMP

BROCKHAMPTON

River Wye

*Not to scale*   ——— Start

Continue the walk down the hill, keeping to the right. Look over the edge on the left from time to time where there are some pleasant glimpses of the river far below. At the bottom of the hill turn left on to a track which comes back along the hillside below the road. This track goes down to the riverside and past a number of small quarries, now overgrown with trees. Were these in use when Hereford was being built? They are convenient to the river and until the end of the 18th century most building stone was shipped by river wherever possible. It would be an easy journey upstream to the heart of Hereford. Pass the small hut on the left and walk on along the track through the trees.

On reaching a long narrow watermeadow, continue for ¼ mile to where there is a track going up the hillside, through the trees. At the bottom of this track, on the right, there is an old willow which has a split trunk and a number of its branches have cracked so that the tips rest on the ground. This is a good example of a crack willow. It is summer flowering, as also is the white willow, from which it can be distinguished by not having white hairs on the underside of its leaves. The cricket bat willow is a hybrid of these two. Walk up the track which ends in the car park.

# MARCLE RIDGE HILL

WALK 28

★

6½ miles (10.5 km)

OS Landranger 149, Pathfinder SO 63/73

The Marcle Ridge is 6 miles south west of Ledbury and 5 miles north of Ross on Wye. The walk starts from a small car park and picnic area provided by the Wye Valley Countryside Service. It is to be found halfway along the Marcle Ridge, and is ½ mile west of Rushall, 1½ miles north west of Sollers Hope and 1½ miles south east of Woolhope (½ mile from the transmitting mast).

The countryside to the north, west and south is a maze of small lanes, so it is best approached from the A449 Ledbury – Ross road. From the crossroads at Much Marcle take the turning at the side of Westons Garage. This will take you past Westons Cider and Perry Mill – so prominently advertised on the sides of the garage. About ¾ mile along this road, at the first crossroads, turn right towards Woolhope. As you go up the hill the mast looms closer. Near the top of the hill turn right (GR: SO 630 347). Continue along the road to reach the car park.

Climb up to the stile at the T junction and walk along the well used path which looks down into the car park. In the third field the path bears right to a stile and then continues on the opposite side of the hedge. Eventually the path comes back over a stile to continue with the hedge on the right. Ahead (½ mile) can be seen the earthworks of Oldbury prehistoric camp, one of the many which crown the hills in these parts. On reaching the track turn right.

Continue on the sunken track down the hill. In ½ mile you pass an old limekiln where the arched fire holes can be clearly seen. On the top, round at the back, the small holes can still be seen where the limestone was put in before firing to make lime for the fields and mortar for building.

At the bottom of the hill walk along the lane ahead. After crossing the stream continue along a lane for 200 yards to the top of the first rise and look on the right for a stile in the hedge. In the field beyond, go straight across to the bottom corner and through a gate. Now follow the hedge and stream on the right to

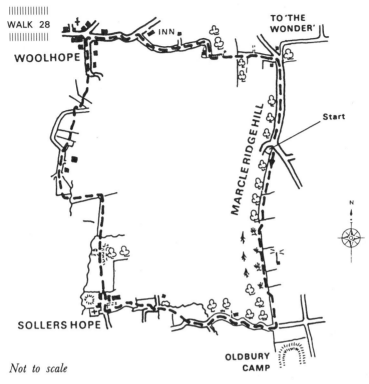

WOOLHOPE

INN

TO 'THE WONDER'

MARCLE RIDGE HILL

Start

N

SOLLERS HOPE

*Not to scale*

OLDBURY CAMP

a lane. Bear left along the lane for 20 yards, passing the end of a barn, to turn right through a gate. In this field turn left, gradually rising to the hedge and fence on the right. In 100 yards go over a fence into the bottom corner of another field. Go along the field, passing the orchard on the right. Opposite the open barns, look for a fence on the left. The way out of the field is over a stile in the far left hand corner, opposite the entrance to the church.

This is Sollers Hope. The early 16th century black and white farmhouse is on the site of the old manor house. Behind the house and next to the church is a prehistoric tump and earth circle. In the early years of Christianity churches were built on top of these earthworks, thereby establishing the superiority of the new religion. Here, as at Kings Caple near the start of Walk 25, the church was built at the side of the sacred site.

Go through the farmyard with the house on the left, and in the field beyond follow the track. On approaching the end of the field there are the remains of a dam across the valley, and the track goes through a gap in the bank. There must have been a large pool on the far side of this bank, long before the time of enclosures. Was this a fish pond or a supply of water for a mill?

89

Just inside the wood there are signs of a track, now grassed over, going round the edge of the hill. Continue straight ahead to a stile which leads into the bottom corner of a field. Keep in the same direction in the next field, with the hedge on the left. Continue for ¼ mile and go into the next field. Here turn left and go down to the corner where there is a new footbridge over the stream. In the next field the stile is 50 yards ahead on the right. From here cross to the far corner of the triangular field and out to a lane. There is an old ford down to the right.

Walk up the lane and at the first left hand bend go straight ahead, through a gate. Follow the hedge on the right until it ends and then go forward to a stile in a fence. Now bear left across the field to a stile in the opposite hedge, 50 yards from the left hand corner. From this stile go straight ahead, past the few remaining trees of an old orchard, to a stile onto the lane. Cross the lane and go over another stile. In the field turn right and go across the end of the field to a stile and footbridge. From the little footbridge bear slightly left to a stile in the hedge opposite. Go straight ahead from this stile, up the bank in front and then walk along the ridge to a gate and so on to a lane. Keep the same direction along the lane into Woolhope.

At the crossroads turn right down the hill on the road to Putley. In ¼ mile, just before reaching the car park of the Butchers Arms, turn right along a lane which winds up the hill. Keep ahead up the track, which eventually turns right along the hillside to a gate. Go through the gate and turn left up the hill next to the wood on the left. As you go you will notice, in the high bank on the left, how the layers of hard limestone, which form the hill, have been pushed up. This is the edge of Woolhope Dome, as described in Walk 30. Keep ahead past another limekiln to a stile in the hedge in front. From here follow the path down through the wood. On leaving the wood by either a hunting gate or the stile, continue across the valley next to the hedge on the left. In the far corner of the field go through a gate and walk up a sunken track. This is a continuation of the old road which started near the Butchers Arms. At the lane turn right.

In 1575 a great portion of the hillside near here slid gently down, burying a church and some houses. It has been known ever since as the Wonder Landslip. Should you wish to extend your walk and visit the site it will entail an extra 1½ miles. To do so, go up the track at the side of the house opposite the gate you came through onto the road, and in ¼ mile turn left along another track. This takes you to what looks like an old quarry but is where the slip started. It travelled downhill and a road goes over where it ended. Return to the lane, continuing up it and along the ridge. The start of the walk is ½ mile ahead.

# HOLME LACY

WALK 29

★

5 miles (8 km)

OS Landranger 149, Pathfinder 45/53

Holme Lacy is a small settlement 4 miles south east of Hereford. It lies on the B4339 road which links the A49 in Hereford to the B4224 near Fownhope. Go along the road opposite the Agricultural College in Holme Lacy towards Bolstone. In ¼ mile turn left, signposted 'Church Road'. Go under the bridge and follow the lane down to the church.

Please leave clear the turning area in front of the church entrance and any gateways. There is sufficient parking space on the grass verge back along the lane towards the sharp bend (GR: SO 568 347).

This walk starts from Holme Lacy church, which lies 1 mile south east of the present village with only the old vicarage standing nearby. This isolated position, on the lowest ground in the parish, raises the question, why here? Look in the adjoining field and you will see some uneven patches – flat areas with hollows in between. These are the remains of an early settlement. There is the site of a moated manor house and a street with a number of house plots. The estate (parish) was well established at the end of the Saxon period with an outlying dependency at Llanwarne, some 6 miles away. Both places had priests, so there was a church here before 1086. As the climate gradually became wetter and colder from the 14th century, old manor houses and low lying fields tended to be abandoned and everybody moved to higher ground, leaving the churches behind.

Walk back along the lane to the sharp bend and keep straight ahead to a gate. In the field beyond, turn left and walk through the meadows by the side of the river. The trees growing in the bank are common alders. They like the moist situation on the riverbank so that they can drink deep and despatch their children by water to a similar place downstream. Charcoal for gunpowder was made from alder wood, so many of the older trees have been coppiced and are now in bush form.

Continue past the road bridge for nearly 1½ miles until you

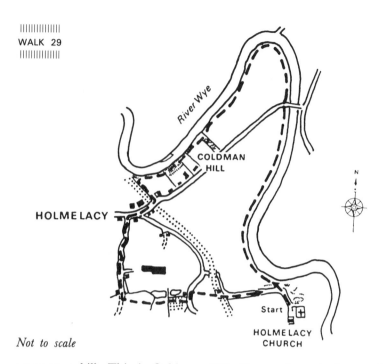

*Not to scale*

come to a hill. This is Coldman Hill. Go up through the small plantation and keep to the right in the field beyond. When you arrive at the top pass through a field with fine views down to the Wye on the right. The path now goes between a high ridge of earth on the left and a steep drop down to the river on the right. Do not bear right down the hillside. In the next field keep near the hedge on the right. In 200 yards, at the first corner, the right of way goes on along the edge of the cliff down the hill. It then returns to arrive back into this field 50 yards ahead, at the second corner. Walk on by the side of the hedge which is just above the old, very overgrown railway which used to run from Hereford to Ross and Monmouth. As you approach the white house you can see the old station down below.

On reaching the road turn right and take great care as you cross the railway bridge, especially at the far end, as there is no pavement. Continue by the Agricultural College with its well laid-out gardens, past Bower Farm. Just beyond the black and white house on the left, turn left. This is the rear entrance to Holme Lacy House. Walk along this drive and when you come to a fork go right, round the corner of a high brick wall. Pass the extensive walled garden on the left and cross a cattle grid at the entrance to the park. A few yards past here turn left through a gate and bear right to go down the valley to the right of the lake.

As you descend you will notice a gigantic tree on the left. On measuring its trunk 5 ft from the ground, it was found to be just over 30 ft in circumference. A rough estimate for an oak tree, growing in the open, is that it starts at the rate of one inch in six months and at 360 inches would take four to five years to add a further inch to its girth. After some complex calculations it is suggested that this tree might have been a young sapling when Joan of Arc was burnt, some 550 years ago.

Holme Lacy House was built by the second Viscount Scudamore in the late 17th century and is in the most magnificent setting that could be imagined. With views of distant wooded hills across spacious lawns and lakes, it is the interior which is breathtaking. What a pity that the house is not open to the public! Stripped of all furniture and its best woodwork, it would be thrilling to see the plaster ceilings, which are amongst the finest in the country. The first Lord Scudamore is today remembered for having propagated and made popular the famous cider apple called Redsteak. As a result Herefordshire has been the centre for British cidermaking for over three centures, despite what they say in Devon and Somerset! During the 18th century tens of thousands of hogsheads of cider were made, some being exported to Bristol and London, where it was considered equal to any French wine. After the Napoleonic Wars there was a temporary decline in quality and quantity and it became the 'make-wage' for farm labourers. At the turn of the century, factories grew up in and around Hereford, three of which survive today – Bulmers, Symonds and Westons. There is a cider museum in Hereford which is worth a visit.

Walk on past the lakes to a gate into an orchard. Keep straight ahead along the bottom of the orchard and when the trees end go down to a gate on to the road beyond. Turn left along the road past the old school house and in a few yards go over a stile on the right. Cross the field aiming to the right of the farm buildings ahead. Go over the old railway to the road and keep straight ahead to the car.

# HAUGH WOOD

WALK 30

★

4 miles (6.5 km)

OS Landranger 149, Pathfinder 45/53

Haugh (pronounced Hoff or Huff) Wood is 4 miles south east of
Hereford. It lies on both sides of the road between Mordiford and
Woolhope, at about the halfway point.

Cars can be parked at the Forestry Commission car park at the
highest point in the wood (GR: SO 592 365). There is a stone
pillar on the left as you enter the car park. From here you can
purchase a leaflet which describes a most interesting forest trail.

At the end of the Ordovician era (440 million years ago) the
Silurian limestones and shales were laid down at the bottom of
shallow seas. These were later folded and Devonian old red
sandstone (ORS) laid down on top. Since then erosion has
removed much of the ORS leaving the tops of the underlying folds
exposed. These in turn are now being weathered. Because the
Silurian rocks are harder they have worn away slower. This walk
starts on the lowest layer, the Cambrian sandstones (at least 500
million years old) and goes over a number of different Silurian
rocks.

Walk 28 is entirely on Silurian limetones and shales and Walk
20 is on the old red sandstone, which forms most of the
Herefordshire plain.

Leave the car park by the main entrance and cross the road to
enter the southern half of the wood along a wide forest road. As
you go along through the wood keep a look out on the ground for
streams of ants being very busy. Many ants have no sting but
defend themselves by squirting formic acid at their attackers.
Sometimes they can be seen carrying long slivers of wood ten
times their own length. Think of carrying a floorboard 60 ft long
over rough ground – between your teeth!

Pass the foresters' huts and in 100 yards fork left. Follow this
forest road, as it winds its way through the woods, for nearly
½ mile to a T junction and turn right. Continue for ¾ mile and
at the T junction a short diversion is most rewarding. Walk up the
hill for a few yards to a major junction where there is a seat with

94

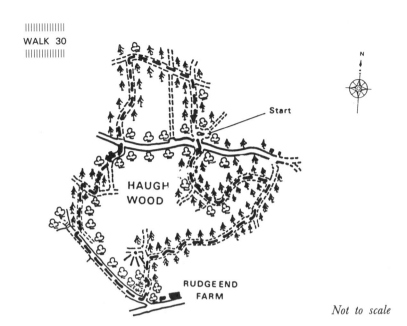

Start

HAUGH
WOOD

RUDGE END
FARM

*Not to scale*

a fine view. Fownhope is just beyond the hill in front. To continue the walk go down the hill and at the track at the bottom turn right.

On the right is the Rudge End Quarry Nature Reserve, managed by the Herefordshire and Radnorshire Nature Trust Ltd. These nature trusts are to be found in all counties. They do a fine job ensuring the survival of wildlife and preserving a balance between conservation and the needs of man for food production, recreation and housing. They also bring to the notice of owners, users and planners of land the need for conservation, so that they do not unwittingly destroy what we need to conserve.

Follow the farm track along the bottom of the wood for nearly ½ mile to where it enters the wood. A few yards before reaching the cattle grid look on the right, behind a nut bush, for a small gate into the wood. Go 5 yards into the wood and turn left. Follow this path until it emerges onto a forest road. Turn right and go up the hill. In 100 yards, before reaching the top of the slope, look on the left for an old, partly overgrown, forest road which turns back along the hillside. Go along here and eventually curve up to a wide forest road. In 50 yards pass round a barrier and follow the lane past some cottages out to the main road, which you cross. Now follow the forest road. There are many smashed snail shells to be seen. The snails live in the damp ditches and banks, mostly on the right. The birds find them but have to bring them out to where there is a hard surface before they can get at the snails inside the shells.

In ½ mile at a T junction turn right up to a wide crossing of forest roads. There are seats at all pleasant viewpoints where you can see some of the geology of the district. You are now on the Woolhope Dome, which is made of a hard rock. All round the Dome are layers of softer rocks which have been thrust up on edge and then worn down. Further out there are rings of harder rocks. The Dome is the oldest rock and the wooded ring is the youngest.

From the track you came up turn right back to the car.

*Common Oak*